Heaven: Better By Far

Heaven:
Better By Far

J. Oswald Sanders

DISCOVERY HOUSE
PUBLISHERS®

Feeding the Soul with the Word of God

Heaven: Better By Far
© 1993 by Discovery House Publishers. All rights reserved.

Discovery House Publishers is affiliated with RBC Ministries, Grand Rapids, Michigan 49512

Discovery House books are distributed to the trade exclusively by Barbour Publishing, Inc., Uhrichsville, Ohio 44683

Library of Congress Cataloging-in-Publishing Data

Sanders, J. Oswald (John Oswald), 1902–1992
    Heaven : better by far / J. Oswald Sanders.
        p.   cm.

    ISBN 0-929239-72-5

    1. Heaven—Christianity. 2. Heaven—biblical teaching.
I. Title.
BT846.2.S26   1993
232'.24—dc20   93–31267
                                             CIP

Printed in the United States of America

09 10 / CHG / 17 16 15 14

CONTENTS

Foreword

During a conversation with the author in November 1991, Oswald Sanders mentioned that he was in the process of completing a manuscript on heaven. He said that his reason for writing a book on this subject was that it would be his next home and he expected to be there relatively soon. At that time, Sanders was 89 years old and in good health. He preached over 300 times that year and was going strong, but he knew the time of his homegoing was near. Eleven months later, a week after his 90th birthday, the Lord took him quietly in his sleep.

Dr. Sanders was one of the last of a great generation of Bible teachers and we are the richer for having been the heirs of his ministry for seventy years. He wrote over 40 books and preached thousands of times. His ministry spanned the world and he was loved by all who knew him.

Someone has said that heaven is a prepared place for a prepared people. Oswald Sanders was prepared and the glory of heaven is now his—a glory so magnificent even the apostle Paul found it difficult to describe (2 Cor. 12:1–6). And while we wait to join him in the supreme ecstasy of seeing Him "who sits on the throne" (Rev. 7:10), we have the opportunity to share through these pages what Dr. Sanders learned of the place that is the believer's destiny—and the Person who is our hope.

Robert K. DeVries
Publisher

Introduction

Some little time ago, it occurred to me that, as I was getting perilously close to becoming a nonagenarian and my next major stop would be heaven, I had better become more acquainted with my future home! So I began a study of that theme for my own personal profit.

However, as I talked about the subject, I discovered that few whom I asked had ever heard a sermon about it. I visited a reputable evangelical bookstore, but not a book on heaven was to be found there! In view of the importance of the subject for every believer and the paucity of its treatment from the pulpit and in book form, I decided to take up my pen.

Dr. Thomas Dick has commented that the greater part of Christians rest content with the vaguest and most incorrect ideas of heaven, and talk and write in so loose and figurative a manner as to convey no rational or definite conception.

In our dollar-oriented and materialistic world, the subject of heaven has been relegated to the back burner. It is seldom a topic of conversation and seldom gains a place in newspapers or television programs. A reporter at an airport terminal posed this question to thirty people: "Do you know for certain that you will go to heaven when you leave this world?" He met with a unanimous negative response.

Of course this is a subject on which one can write only with reserve, for most of what we know about heaven is not couched in categorical terms, but has been determined in a negative manner. We know much more about what will *not* be there than about what *will* be there. Indeed, without revelation we can know *nothing* about the world to come. All else is pure speculation.

But to one who has unshakable confidence in the complete inspiration and final authority of the Bible, while it does not tell us all we would *like* to know about heaven, it does reveal all we *need* to know. And the picture it paints is so glorious as to leave us breathless in wonder.

In a recent issue of *Living Today*, the official publication of the Presbyterian Church of Australia, the question was posed: "What is the basis for your hope of heaven?" The following were the most popular responses:

I have always lived a good life.

I have been a good family person.

I'm not as bad as the person down the street.

I have always tried to be kind to everyone.

An analysis of the answers showed the prevailing opinion to be, "good people go to heaven." [1]

A recent Gallup Poll disclosed that more Americans than ever before believe in heaven and hell. Seventy-two percent believe their own chances of arriving there are good or excellent. Sixty percent believe in hell, but only four percent think they will end there.

The increasing exposure of our youth to scientific influence with an atheistic bias has resulted in emphasis being placed almost exclusively on this world. The subject of the hereafter is relegated to the background, if indeed it is mentioned by young people at all. The current spate of books on near-death experiences has created a temporary revival of interest in the afterlife, but this seldom seems to lead to the Scriptures. One of the tragic consequences of this famine of truly scriptural teaching about heaven is that the vacuum created is being filled by the erroneous teachings of advocates of the occult, the New Age movement, and Eastern religions. The church is paying dearly for this neglect.

When Paul "was caught up to the third heaven," to "paradise," he heard "inexpressible things, things that man is not permitted to tell" (2 Cor. 12:2–4). Obviously this experience was more glorious and wonderful than he was able to express in the limitations of our finite human language. Accordingly, much of what is revealed about heaven is couched in highly figurative and allegorical language, which cannot be interpreted by the canons of flat prose, and I have sought to keep this in mind, with undue spiritualization.

I have chosen the title, *Heaven: Better By Far*, because, from the biblical description, the highest and holiest and most joyous experiences of earth will be far exceeded by the realities of heaven.

Because the very subject of heaven arouses so many questions in one's mind, I have adopted a question-and-answer format in the book. Although this precludes a consistently consecutive development of the subject, it may be more helpful from a practical point of view. In addition, there are many themes relating to heaven that are not discussed in this volume, and for them the reader can refer to more exhaustive treatments.

I would draw attention to the fact that any italicizing in the texts of Scripture quoted in the book is mine.

As a result of being immersed in this study for a considerable length of time, the magnitude and splendor of God's plan for our future has quickened my anticipation and deepened my wonder and thanksgiving.

J. Oswald Sanders

ONE

Death—Enemy or Benefactor?

Is joyous anticipation of heaven a valid exercise?
What are some myths about heaven?
In what sense is heaven "better by far"?
Is there life after death?
Death—enemy or benefactor?
What is death anyway?

Is joyous anticipation of heaven a valid exercise?
"For to me, to live is Christ and to die is gain. If I am
to go on living in the body, this will mean fruitful labor for me. Yet what shall I choose? I do not know! I
am torn between the two: *I desire to depart and be with
Christ, which is better by far* . . . ."
Philippians 1:21–23

Apparently Paul would return an affirmative answer to my question above, although he did opt in favor of remaining in the body because he judged that
would be in the best interests of the Philippian Christians.

There is every reason for the believer to look forward to the future with joyous anticipation, whether
for him or her it holds the second advent of the Lord,

or in the alternative, entering through the portals of our heavenly home by way of death. That is not mere wishful thinking or a form of escapism, but a well-founded confidence. We have reason to share Paul's conviction that to be with Christ is better by far than anything we can possibly conceive.

There is no reason why the closing years of our lives should not be cheered and brightened by contemplating the undreamed of felicity that awaits the bride of Christ in heaven. And why should we not rejoice in the thought of the absence from life of all that now saddens or frustrates us?—for this is what our Lord assures us lies ahead.

"The consideration of heaven is no mere spiritual luxury," writes W. H. Griffith Thomas, "no mere intellectual dissipation, no imaginative reverie, but is really and definitely practicable and suitable for the robust thinker and worker, as well as for the contemplative mystic, and has real bearing on our daily life."

Indeed, it is very probable that many who are now blasé about the thought of heaven will be filled with regret that they did not spend more time in thinking of it and making better preparation for it. The quality of our life and service here has a very real bearing on our felicity and reward there.

In our materialistic age, however, it is out of fashion to spend time anticipating the glories of heaven— perhaps in part because of the uninviting manner in which the occupations of heaven have been portrayed. Many prefer to be involved in the pressing social issues of the day and to make *this world* a better place to live in. This is understandable. But should we not choose both/and, not either/or? In this connection, Dr. J. H. Jowett wrote autobiographically, "I felt with some other young reformers that instead of singing about the glories of Christ, I would engage the interest of my congregation in conditions in the slums, etc., and concentrate on bettering the life that is. *But I discovered that no man works less eagerly for the slums because now and then he has a vision of the City of God.*"

A study of history, both secular and sacred, reveals that the Christians who have effected the most significant social change have been those who have been gripped by "the powers of the coming age" (Heb. 6:5). Such contemplation quickens the social conscience of the compassionate Christian and adds another dimension to his or her service. The influence of such people in the community is beneficent, like that of salt.

From the record of the lives of the Old Testament saints who made their way into God's Hall of Fame (Heb. 11), we can learn much of profit as we consider their outlook on the world to come.

> All these people were still living by faith when they died. They did not receive the things promised; they only saw them and welcomed them from a distance. And they admitted that they were aliens and strangers on earth. People who say such things show that they are looking for a country of their own. If they had been thinking of the country they had left, they would have had opportunity to return. *Instead, they were longing for a better country—a heavenly one.*
>
> *Hebrews 11:13–16*

Even the Greek philosophers, pagan though they were, saw value in spending time in contemplation of the future life. In his *Phaedo*, Plato puts into the mouth of Socrates, who is talking with his friends and disciples shortly before he drinks the hemlock cup, "Perhaps it most becoming for one who is about to travel there, to inquire and speculate about the journey thither, what kind we think it is. What else can one do?"

Socrates could do no more than speculate about his future, but we can know with certainty. When we, Scripture in hand, contemplate the future, the text enables us to view things, not from the perspective of this smoggy world, but from that of a holy God. The "comfort of the Scriptures" relieves the poignancy of bereavement and enables us to cope with the exigencies of this life. It also provides a powerful motive to lay up treasure in heaven, rather than on earth.

What are some myths about heaven?
"Have nothing to do with godless myths. . . ."
1 Timothy 4:7

Before answering this question, it is necessary to define what we mean when we speak of heaven. One dictionary definition is, "The abode of God, and of the righteous, after death."

The Greek word translated "heaven" is used in three ways in the Bible. It refers to:

1. The *aerial* or atmospheric heavens—a cosmological usage. These form one of the primeval divisions of the universe, as in Genesis 1:1: "In the beginning God created the heavens and the earth."

2. The *sidereal* or starry heavens, of which our generation has a grander conception than any before.

And yet, with all our greatly increased knowledge, we are only paddling around on the shores of immensity. The starry heavens have been described as "more like infinity than anything we know—an emblem in space and time of God's eternal life, just as a rainbow is an emblem of His everlasting covenant."[4] Immense as these heavens are, Solomon cut them down to size when he said of them, "The heavens, even the highest heaven, cannot contain you" (1 Kings 8:27).

3. *The eternal abode of God*, as used in the Lord's Prayer: "Our Father in heaven." It is here that the redeemed and the unfallen angels will be able to share the life of God and the felicity of the Redeemer. It was from this heaven that the preexistent Christ descended in order to assume our human nature—always with a view to our redemption. When He ascended, "He passed through the heavens" (Heb. 4:14 NKJV). As a result and reward for His redemptive work, He was "exalted to the right hand of God" (Acts 2:33). These expressions do not signify palatial location, but rather a regal function.[5] In His ascension, Jesus was only resuming the exalted position He had enjoyed from all eternity.

Now to answer our question for this segment.

The prevalence of metaphorical and symbolic language in the biblical references to heaven has given rise to some strange misconceptions and myths. The most grotesque of these have come from those who insist on interpreting poetic speech according to the canons of prose, when it is plain from the context that such an interpretation cannot be sustained. Here are some of the more common distortions:

- *That heaven's main occupation* will be sitting on a cloud, plucking the strings of a golden harp. This concept is common in popular thought and is rightly rejected.
- *That everything in heaven will be bland,* offering no challenge—nothing to look forward to with keen anticipation. Nothing could be further from the truth about heaven as it is revealed in Scripture, as we shall see.
- *That life in heaven will consist largely of rest and contemplation,* without absorbing occupation. To the activist on earth, perpetual rest would seem more like hell than heaven. Such a life would inevitably issue in frustration, and boredom. In any case, *rest* in biblical terms means anything but lounging around. It signifies not rest *from* activity but rest *in* activity.

F. W. H. Myers, author of the magnificent poem *Saint Paul,* is reputed to have asked a woman whose daughter had died what she supposed had happened to her daughter's soul. "Oh, I suppose she is enjoying eternal bliss," was the reply, "but I wish you wouldn't speak to me of such unpleasant subjects." Another sad misconception.

- *That longing for heaven is weakness and a form of escapism.* But is not the shoe really on the other foot? Since there *is* a life to come of weal or woe, is it not the absence of such longing and anticipation that is escapism? Is not the prospect of meeting and being with the Lord something to anticipate with pleasure?
- *That there will be nothing interesting to do in heaven.* This is a groundless fear. One of heaven's rewards for faithful service on earth, according to Christ's words, will be the allocation of various spheres of authority.

Hear the words of His illustration:

> A man of noble birth went to a distant country. . . .
> Then he sent for the servants to whom he had given the
> money, in order to find out what they had gained with
> it.
> The first one came and said, "Sir, your mina has
> earned ten more."
> "Well done, my good servant!" his master replied.
> "Because you have been trustworthy in a very small
> matter, *take charge of ten cities.*"
> The second came and said, "Sir, your mina has
> earned five more."
> His master answered, *"You take charge of five cities."*
>
> *Luke 19:12–19*

That doesn't sound like doing nothing! But it should
be noted that the delegated responsibility in heaven
is in proportion to the faithful discharge of responsibilities on earth. Heaven is not a resort for the lazy or
listless. Jesus presented His Father as a God of activity. "My Father is always at his work," Jesus declared
(John 5:17), and He will have plenty of congenial
work for us to do.

• *That the music of heaven will be dull, heavy, and repeti-
tive.* The brilliant American humorist Mark Twain
pilloried the music of heaven as very boring. "It goes
on all day long and every day, during a stretch of
twelve hours," he wrote. "The singing is of hymns
alone, nay, it is of one hymn alone. The words are always the same; in number they are only about a doz-
en; there is no rhyme, there is no poetry. . . ." [6] In this
appraisal of the singing of heaven, the brilliant
though apparently unregenerate cynic is guilty of an
inexcusable fault in a man of letters—interpreting an

apocalyptic and obviously symbolic passage as though it were prose. It will be "a *new* song" that is sung. "Behold, I make all things new," were the Master's words.

Bertrand Russell shared Mark Twain's viewpoint. He shrank from the thought of an endless life in the future, because it would be so boring. But was he not thereby revealing the quality of his own life on earth? To him John Newton's famous hymn, *Amazing Grace*, would bring no satisfaction.

> When we've been there ten thousand years,
>   Bright shining as the sun,
> We've no less days to sing God's praise,
>   Than when we'd first begun.

Lovers are never bored in each other's company! In heaven we will be with Him "Whom having not seen, [we] love; in whom, though now [we] see him not, yet believing, [we] rejoice with joy unspeakable and full of glory" (1 Peter 1:8 KJV).

• *That Peter guards the pearly gates.* This is pure fantasy and without biblical support. It arises from a misinterpretation of Matthew 16:18–19.

• *That we become angels,* wearing halos and wings. There is not a shred of scriptural support for these notions.

In what sense is heaven "better by far"?

"If I am to go on living in the body, this will mean fruitful labor for me. Yet what shall I choose? I do not know! I am torn between the two: I desire to depart and be with Christ, which is better by far; but it is more necessary for you that I remain in the body."

Philippians 1:22–24

Paul was torn between a sense of pastoral responsibility and the desire for personal enjoyment and satisfaction. He was in no doubt as to which was better. Had he not had a foretaste of heaven? In an autobiographical reference he wrote:

> I know a man in Christ who fourteen years ago was caught up to the third heaven. Whether it was in the body or out of the body I do not know—God knows. And I know that this man . . . was caught up to paradise. He heard inexpressible things, things that man is not permitted to tell.
>
> *2 Corinthians 12:2–4*

So when Paul said that heaven was better by far, he was speaking from experience. When the hour of his martyrdom drew near, he faced it with a cheerful serenity and sublime assurance. There was no fear or reluctance.

> For I am already being poured out like a drink offering, and the time has come for my departure. I have fought the good fight, I have finished the race, I have kept the faith. Now there is in store for me the crown of righteousness, which the Lord, the righteous Judge, will award to me on that day. . . .
>
> *2 Timothy 4:6–8*

Early historians remarked on the courage and joy with which the Christians faced cruel death. In A.D. 125, in a letter to a friend, Aristides described "a new religion called Christianity." "If any righteous man among the Christians passes from this world, they rejoice, and offer thanks to God; and they escort the body with songs of thanksgiving, as if he were setting out from one place to another nearby."

Those suffering saints attained a wholesome and triumphant approach to the reality of death, because they had believed in and experienced the power of Christ's resurrection and they cherished a wholesome confidence that a joyous heaven awaited them. The stark contrast between their joy and triumph and the hopeless mourning and wailing of their pagan contemporaries in the presence of death proved a powerful evangelistic agency.

The atheist is in no better position than the pagan. When Huxley's mother died, this was all he could write to his sister: "My dearest sister, I offer you no consolation, for I know of none. There are things which each must bear as best he may with the strength that has been allotted to him."

Heaven is so much better than the best experiences of earth, that one can summarize only a few of its benefits and blessings:

• We will enjoy eternal life in the immediate presence of the triune God.
• All that diminishes the quality of life on earth will be banished from heaven.
• The heights of joy we have experienced on earth will be eclipsed in heaven.
• We will be "saved to sin no more." Failure and its consequences will be a thing of the past.
• No more will we be subject to temptations from the world, the flesh, and the devil.
• Knowledge will no longer be limited.
• Limitations of the body will hamper us no more.
• Everything that would enrich our lives will be available.

• Reunion with loved ones and the formation of new relationships will make heaven a wonderful place of fellowship.
• Heaven's music will far surpass earth's finest achievements in that realm.
• There will be full satisfaction for every holy and wholesome longing and aspiration.
In short, HEAVEN IS BETTER BY FAR.

> Face to face with Christ my Savior,
> Face to face what will it be
> When with rapture I behold Him,
> Jesus Christ, who died for me.

Is there life after death?
"If a man dies, will he live again?"

Job 14:14

> One question more than all others
> From thoughtful minds implores reply;
> It is breathed from star and pall,
> What fate awaits us when we die?

In spite of Paul's confident assurance to the believers at Philippi—and to us—that "For to me, to live is Christ and *to die is gain*" (1:21), and that "to depart and be with Christ . . . is *better by far*" (1:23), even among Christians there is a widespread fear of the lonely experience of death. Or perhaps it may be fear of the process of dying rather than fear of death itself. There are many experiences in life that are within our control, but this is something that is inevitable and eludes our grasp.

In order to alleviate the grim reality of death, we resort to euphemisms to gild it. The mortuary or morgue of former days is now the funeral home. The coffin is a casket. Forest Lawn Memorial Cemetery in Los Angeles has been made very attractive and has even been popularized as a desirable venue for weddings. Soft music helps to relieve the poignancy of parting. But death still remains death and is a topic of conversation to be avoided studiously.

It is related of Philip Neri, one of the great Italian characters of the sixteenth century, that once, as he was walking down a street of his native Florence, he saw coming toward him a lad he knew who was clearly in the midst of some happy experience. His joy showed itself in his face and in his gait. As they met, the older man asked the youth what was the occasion of his obvious gladness. Well, the boy explained, he had just completed his course in the university and received his degree. Those years of toil were over, and life was to begin.

"Very good," said the old man, "and what next?" The boy replied that he was even then on his way to the office of the city's leading lawyers to begin the study of law in preparation for his career. "Very good," said the old man, "and what then?" Well, the boy answered, he intended to win fame and wealth and to achieve a great name in Florence. "I hope so," said the old man, "and what then?" Well, said the lad, he supposed it would be with him as with all men. Life at last must come to its end. "Yes, indeed," said the old man, "and what next?" The lad made no answer, and they went their ways, the boy solemn now and thinking on the inevitable question: "When this life is over, what next? Is there a life beyond?"

To the question, If a man dies, will he live again? there are different answers from different groups. The *rationalist* Thomas Hobbes, when facing death, said, "I am taking a fearful leap into the dark." The *materialist* sees nothing more in human beings than mere flesh and blood. They come from earth and return to earth. They have no future. *Scientists* can throw no light on the problem, nor should we expect them to, for science deals only with things that can be perceived with our senses. Of things beyond experience science knows nothing authoritative. The *agnostic* does not believe in any divine revelation and maintains that no one knows or can know what lies beyond death.

The concept of a heaven after death is not a peculiarly Christian idea. Among men and women both pagan and sophisticated there is an inborn desire for immortality. Evidence of this innate longing is present among most primitive peoples, as is a belief in existence after death. While these ideas are not necessarily a proof of certain survival, they are evidence of an almost universal belief in immortality that has to be accounted for.

One common feature of these concepts is that they envisage this present life as continuing indefinitely after death, together with the gratification of all physical desires. Another common thought among many groups is that in the next life there will be reward for virtue, compensation for suffering, and punishment for wrongdoing. Is this universal desire and conviction merely a mirage, or does it have its roots in reality?

Some regard this question as irrelevant in the space age. The thought of a life of unceasing bliss after death is considered unrealistic and ridiculous. Sitting on a cloud strumming a golden harp is anything but an alluring prospect. Even among Christians, the popular gospel of "health, wealth, and success" in this life has served to dim any desire for heaven. Heaven can be here and now.

But belief in life after death is inherent in humankind's very constitution, for God "has also set eternity in the hearts of men" (Eccl. 3:11).

The hope of life after death and related themes was prominent in both conversation and literature a century ago, but today the here and now so engrosses the attention of most people that the word *immortality* is not in their vocabularies. Heaven and hell have become increasingly rare notes in contemporary preaching, and this is reflected in the popular attitude.

There has, however, in recent times been a slight reversal of this trend, perhaps as a spin-off from the prevalence of crime, violence, and war in society. The popularity of Eastern religions and the rapid increase in occult activity have also stimulated interest in this area. In addition, curiosity has been aroused in the formerly skeptical by the widespread claims of people who had been classed as clinically dead but were brought back to life, that they had had happy "out-of-body" experiences while "dead."

Among the Greek philosophers who argued for the indestructibility of the soul, Cicero claimed that there is in the mind of human beings a certain presentiment of immortality, which takes the deepest root and is most discoverable in the greatest geniuses and the most exalted souls.

In his *Cato*, Joseph Addison writes:

It must be so! Plato, thou reasonest well,
Else whence this pleasing hope, this fond desire,
This longing after immortality?
Or whence this secret dread and inward horror
Of falling into naught? Why shrinks the soul
Back on herself and startles at destruction?
'Tis the divinity that stirs within us;
'Tis heaven itself that points out a hereafter
And intimates eternity to man. [7]

When to this weight of extrabiblical evidence for immortality is added the clear and unequivocal assertions of the infallible Word of God, we can affirm with confidence that *there is indeed life after death.*

The pessimistic and hopeless outlook of a great writer on the life beyond contrasts strangely with the optimistic hope of the Christian. When he was dying, Bertrand Russell the atheist said, "There is a darkness without, and when I die there will be darkness within. There is no splendor, no vastness anywhere, only triviality for a moment and then, nothing."

But when Harriet Beecher Stowe, author of the celebrated *Uncle Tom's Cabin,* was confronted with her dearly loved son Henry's death, she said, "Jesus will give me back my loved one whom He is educating in a far higher sphere than I proposed."

Why be afraid of death as though your life was breath?
Death but anoints your eyes with clay. O glad surprise!
Is sleep a thing you dread? Yet sleeping you are dead
Till you awake and rise, here or beyond the skies.

Death—enemy or benefactor?
"O death, where is thy sting? O grave, where is thy victory? The sting of death is sin. . . ."
1 Corinthians 15:55–56 KJV

27

This optimistic verse embraces two of the most unpopular words in the English language—*death* and *grave*. Paul has in mind the lethal and excruciatingly painful sting of the scorpion, which he equates with sin in its painful results. Through the instrumentality of sin, death and the grave have for millennia held cruel sway over the human race. The author of the letter to the Hebrews refers to "those who all their lives were held in slavery by their fear of death" (2:15).

In the powerful polemic of 1 Corinthians 15, Paul argues that in His resurrection, Christ extracted death's sting and robbed the grave of its transient triumph. Even before His resurrection Jesus spoiled the funerals He attended. The grave's victory was reversed, and death's sting neutralized. When Jesus rose from the dead, Satan suffered a stupendous defeat from which he will never recover.

The potent verse quoted above throws down a double challenge to death and the grave. Since the resurrection of Christ, no Christian has any grounds for fearing the changes death may bring. Where is now the nameless dread that has haunted the hearts of people since that fateful day in Eden?

The martyrdom in 1934 of John and Betty Stam, missionaries of the China Inland Mission, shook the entire Christian world. They were beheaded by Chinese bandits. John had been prepared somewhat for martyrdom by a poem sent to him while he was in language school. It was written about the martyrdom of another missionary at the hands of bandits in North China. When, gun in hand, they asked their prisoner if he were not afraid, he answered, "No! If you shoot, I go straight to heaven!"

The poem was written by E. H. Hamilton, also a missionary to China, and it proved very meaningful to John.

> Afraid? Of what?
> Afraid to see the Savior's face,
> To hear His welcome and to trace
> The glory gleam from words of grace?
> Afraid—of that?
>
> Afraid? Of what?
> A flash, a crash, a pierced heart;
> Darkness, light, O heaven's art!
> A wound of His counterpart,
> Afraid—of that?
>
> Afraid? Of what?
> To do by death what life could not—
> Baptize with blood a stony plot,
> Till souls shall blossom from that spot?
> Afraid—of that?

What is death anyway?

How may it be defined? In a lecture reported in the London *Times* of December 12, 1967, Dr. Henry Beecher proposed three helpful medical definitions:[8]

Death occurs:

1. The moment at which irreversible destruction of brain matter, with no possibility of regaining consciousness, is conclusively determined.

2. The moment at which spontaneous heartbeat cannot be restored.

3. The moment "brain death" is established by the electroencephalogram.

Perhaps the simplest definition from the religious point of view is *separation from the source of life.*

Scripture differentiates three types of death:

Physical—the separation of the body from the soul and the spirit.

Spiritual—the separation of soul and spirit from God.

Eternal—spiritual death made permanent. "This is the second death" (Rev. 21:8).

But Jesus taught His disciples that, for a believer, the cessation of life is not "death." He reserved that awesome word for a meaning of infinitely deeper import and insisted on calling the death of a believer "sleep."

> Before going to the tomb of Lazarus He said to His disciples,
> "Our friend Lazarus has fallen asleep; but I am going there to wake him up."
> His disciples replied, "Lord, if he sleeps, he will get better." Jesus had been speaking of his death, but his disciples thought he meant natural sleep.
> So then he told them plainly, "Lazarus is dead. . . ."
>
> *John 11:11–14*

The disciples were obtuse in not realizing that He was not talking about repose in sleep; but since they persisted in their misconception, Jesus put it in plain language.

In a fine sermon, Dr. J. H. Jowett of Birmingham, England, pointed out that Jesus did more than "sleep." "Christ *died* for our sins" (1 Cor. 15:3). On Calvary He experienced the physical cessation we term death. But for Him, as for no other, death held vast and tragic implications. Many of His followers endured the excruciating suffering of crucifixion as He did. But they did not die. They only slept.

The agony and anguish of the cross, the desolation arising from being forsaken by His Father, the crushing weight of a world's sin—*this was death*—the horror of black darkness, the midnight of the soul. [9] Jesus died in order that believers might only sleep.

Understanding this should banish the fear of death, the one experience over which we have no control. To many, however, it is not so much death's darkness they fear, but the process of dying, and what may be ahead after that. For them, this is the disturbing factor.

> . . . the dread of something after death,
> The undiscover'd country from whose bourn
> No traveller returns. . . .
>
> *Hamlet III 1, 78–80*

In earlier years it was in the home that births and deaths took place. They were just part of normal family life and were accepted as such. These events were the everyday topics of conversation. Now they take place, not in the home but in the hospital. Now these intimate family happenings are so segregated that many men and women have no experience of contact with dying and death until mid-life. These things are thus remote from real life, and that makes the stark reality more difficult to face when it does come. Death has become an unacceptable subject of conversation.

However, death should not be viewed as a *terminus* but as a tunnel leading into an ampler and incredibly more wonderful and beautiful world. The death of a believer is a transition, not a final condition. It is helpful to remember, too, that it is only the earthly body that is adversely affected by death.

experiences here is only a taste of heaven. As we live now in the heavenlies, we are merely tasting the glories of the life to come. To us heaven is now a sphere where we live under God's rule and His Spirit's blessing. One day it will also be a place where we will walk in our glorified bodies. [12]

John Mac Arthur, Jr.

TWO

A Place or a State?

Will we know one another in heaven?
Is heaven a place or a state of mind?
Can the living communicate with the dead?
Where do I go when I die?
Is there such a place as purgatory?
What of infants and the mentally retarded?

Will we know one another in heaven?
". . . many will come from the east and the west, and will take their places at the feast with Abraham, Isaac, and Jacob. . . ."

Matthew 8:11

To many, this is the paramount question about life after death. Uncertainty as to the answer has clouded the anticipation of heaven for some. It would be no blissful place for them if they were unable to recognize friends and loved ones of the past. One of the anticipatory joys of heaven is the prospect of reunion. Our question has been expressed poignantly in verse:

> When the holy angels meet us
> As we go to join their band,

> Shall we know the friends that greet us
> In the glorious spirit-land?
>
> Shall we see the same eyes shining
> On us as in days of yore?
> Shall we feel their dear arms twining
> Fondly round us as before?
> Shall we know each other there?

To that question J. H. Bavinck gives the following confident answer, an answer that has abundant support in Scripture: "The hope to see one another in heaven is entirely natural, genuinely human and in harmony with Scripture." [13] Life in heaven will bring enrichment, not impoverishment. The author George Mac Donald once posed the wry question, "Shall we be greater fools in Paradise than we are here?"

There is no Scripture passage that suggests the abolition of all former relationships when we arrive in heaven. In a letter to Canon Barry, Sir William Robertson Nicoll, the noted religious editor, referring to the poet Robert Browning's views on this subject said: "What I gathered from Browning ... was that our personalities are distinct in the next world, and that a pure and holy love between individuals in this life is a creation of God, and will live on in the next." [14]

It is the essential element of personality that will persist after death, not the temporary "tent" in which it is housed on this earth. The body is destined to return to dust, but the inward man, the spirit, lives on, and its identity with the body is not breached.

Angels have no bodies, and yet they exist and act as distinct personalities. If angels who have no bodies are able to recognize one another, why should this not be possible for believers? In Daniel 9:21 and 10:13 it is recorded that Michael the archangel came to the assistance of his colleague Gabriel, when the latter was hindered in his mission by satanic agencies. If angels, why not men and women?

The restoration of sundered relationships is clearly envisaged in 1 Thessalonians 4:15–17.

> . . . we who are still alive, who are left till the coming of the Lord, will certainly not precede those who have fallen asleep. For the Lord himself will come down from heaven, with a loud command, with the voice of the archangel and with the trumpet call of God, and the dead in Christ will rise first. After that, *we who are still alive and are left will be caught up together with them* in the clouds to meet the Lord in the air. And so we will be with the Lord forever.

If there were no recognition in heaven, would not our Lord's parable about the rich man and Lazarus in Luke 16 be devoid of meaning? And in the parable of the dishonest steward, Jesus said to His disciples, "I tell you, use worldly wealth to gain friends for yourselves, so that when it is gone, you will be welcomed into eternal dwellings" (Luke 16:9).

Jesus here envisaged His disciples being welcomed into heaven by those who had been the beneficiaries of their generosity when on earth. Gold invested in God's work is transmuted into souls won to Christ and workers provided for His service. Paul anticipated the joy that would be his when he met in heaven those whom he had been privileged to lead to saving faith in Christ. "For what is our hope, our joy, or the crown in which we will glory in the presence of our Lord Jesus when he comes? Is it not you?" (1 Thess. 2:19).

That passage certainly implies joyous recognition. And there are other biblical instances of reunion and recognition. At the garden tomb, Mary at first did not know Jesus after His resurrection and mistook Him for the gardener. But when she heard the beloved voice saying "Mary!" "she turned toward Him and cried out in Aramaic, 'Rabboni!' (which means Teacher)" (John 20:16). His tone of voice was immediately recognizable.

So it would appear that the holy and spiritual relationships of life on earth will not be severed, but will continue in purified form. Family relationships among believers will not be broken. Death will not destroy our connection with the past.

> O then, what raptured greetings,
>   On Canaan's happy shore,
> What knitting sundered friendships up
>   Where partings are no more.
>
> Then eyes with joy will sparkle
>   That brimmed with tears of late,
> Orphans, no longer fatherless
>   Nor widows desolate.
>
> *Henry Alford*

Of course the strongest argument for the recognition of loved ones in heaven is the appearance of our Lord Himself in His resurrection body, when He said to His disciples, "It is I myself! Touch me and see; a ghost does not have flesh and bones, as you see I have" (Luke 24:39).

Is heaven a place or a state of mind?

"Do not let your hearts be troubled. Trust in God; trust also in me. In my Father's house are many rooms; if it were not so, I would have told you. *I am going there to prepare a place for you.* And if I go and prepare a place for you, I will come back and take you to be with me that you also may be where I am."

John 14:1–3

We encounter difficulties the moment we try to describe in our space-time language events and conditions that are beyond time and space. In the book of Revelation John is struggling to express inexpressible, infinite things in the only vehicle available to him. That is why, under the guidance of the Holy Spirit, he used imperfect earthly terms to describe a heavenly place. When Paul tried to describe his "third heaven" experience, he met the same problem. He could say only that he "heard inexpressible things, things that man is not permitted to tell" (2 Cor. 12:4).

Since this is so, we cannot interpret symbolic writing in a woodenly literal and unimaginative way, as we would a scientific treatise. Nor should we fall into the opposite error of undue spiritualization of the text. Gates of pearl and streets of gold are plainly figurative and should be so interpreted, *but they do stand for something real and substantial.*

In commenting on the thorny problem of interpretation, Alexander Maclaren wrote about physical theories of the future life:

> Some of them read more like a book of travels in this world than forecastings of the next. They may be true or not. It does not matter a whit. *I believe that heaven is a*

place. I believe that the corporeity of our future life is essential to the perfection of it. I believe that Christ wears and will wear for ever a human body. *I believe that that involves locality,* circumstances, external occupations. . . . What is heaven? Likeness to God, love, purity, fellowship with Him.

Heaven is a state in a location somewhere in the great universe of God. It is not a material place that we can locate from down here. The only clue we have as to its whereabouts was given by Jesus when He said to the disciples, "I will come back and take you to be with me *that you also may be where I am"* (John 14:3). Heaven is thus where God is.

Heaven is not *up* in a spatial sense, but the language used conveys the thought that it is infinitely *higher* than anything we know. In His humanity, Jesus could reveal this sublime truth to people only in terms that we could understand.

So, to the question, Is heaven a place? the answer is, Yes, and no. It is not a place in the material sense in which, say, Jerusalem is a place. It will be fundamentally different from our present, space-time environment. To Jesus, heaven was where His Father has His home.

But even this constitutes a problem, for "God is spirit" (John 4:24). Therefore He does not occupy space as we know it. He has no bodily form. Would this not imply that heaven is a state rather than a place?

We, however, are not spirit as the Father is. We will have spiritual bodies. Jesus, too, continues to have His resurrection body, which is somewhere. This would seem to require location.

In the Lord's Prayer there is the petition, "your will be done on earth as it is in heaven" (Matt. 6:10). This, too, would suggest that heaven has a locale, as does the earth (Luke 15:7).

The Ascension of Christ, then, suggests that heaven is a real place. He went somewhere, but the only way in which this place can be described is by the aid of biblical symbols. While heaven is not an actual city, it is *like* a city. All we can say with assurance is what the Bible says it is like and what adverse earthly features will be absent from it.

Can the living communicate with the dead?

"When men tell you to consult mediums and spiritists, who whisper and mutter, should not a people inquire of their God? *Why consult the dead on behalf of the living?*"

Isaiah 8:19

Is it possible to lift the curtain that separates the living from the dead? Can we communicate with those who have died? These are questions that arise, especially in the minds of those who have loved deeply and are now bereaved. They long for some comfort in the realm of the supernatural.

One of the baneful effects of war and widespread natural disasters is a recrudescence of spiritism—the attempt to hold communication with the spirits of the dead through the agency of specially susceptible mediums. In a time of crisis, when a home has an empty chair, such a development is easily understood. Is the loved one happy? Is he or she conscious of what is going on on earth? But the practice of spiritism is roundly condemned in Scripture and is strictly forbidden. "Let no one be found among you . . . who practices divination or sorcery, interprets omens, engages in witchcraft, or casts spells, *or who is a medium or a spiritist or who consults the dead.* Anyone who does these things is detestable to the Lord" (Deut. 18:10–12).

The New Testament is no less vocal in its warnings than the Old. The rise of modern spiritism is one of the predicted signs of the last days, concerning which express warning is given by the Holy Spirit: "The Spirit clearly says that in later times some will abandon the faith and follow deceiving spirits and things taught by demons. Such teachings come through hypocritical liars, whose consciences have been seared as with a hot iron" (1 Tim. 4:1–2).

Some commentators have depicted the Old Testament heroes immortalized in Hebrews 11 as spectators in the race on earth—the cloud of witnesses mentioned in Hebrews 12:1: "Therefore, since we are surrounded by such a great cloud of witnesses . . . let us run with perseverance the race marked out for us."

"Throughout the Epistle [Hebrews], and especially chapter 11," writes Thomas Hewitt, " 'witnesses' invariably means 'one who bears witness,' i.e., one who testifies to a certain fact, and this is the more natural meaning here. In later times it came to mean one who is faithful unto death in his witness-bearing—a martyr. *Nothing can be drawn from this passage as to the relation of the living and the dead.* "[15]

So from an examination of the relevant Scriptures we conclude two things. (1) Attempts by the living to communicate with the dead are expressly forbidden. (2) There is no biblical support for the view that deceased saints take an active, conscious part in the activities of the church militant.

Where do I go when I die?

"Jesus answered him, 'I tell you the truth, today you will be with me in paradise.' "

Luke 23:43

"I desire to depart and be with Christ, which is better by far."

Philippians 1:23

This question is one that every thoughtful person will ask at one time or another. Our sole resort for an authoritative answer is the divinely inspired revelation in the Scriptures. It is characteristic of God's Word that every major doctrine or truth is given extended treatment somewhere in the sacred volume. For example, the Resurrection is discussed at length in 1 Corinthians 15. But there is no such extended treatment in answer to our question above. Nevertheless, we are not left without clear intimations of what lies ahead for the believer in the world to come.

Death involves the separation of the body and the soul (using the latter term to denote the immaterial part of the person). The body disintegrates, but the soul lives on in conscious and personal existence. Some expositors hold the view that in the interval between death and the resurrection, the believer will be in a bodiless state. Others are inclined to think, based on 2 Corinthians 5:1–4, that the believer will be clothed with a "temporary body" until the resurrection, when the spiritual body will be received.

> Now we know that if the earthly tent we live in is destroyed, we have a building from God, an eternal house in heaven, not built by human hands. Meanwhile we groan, longing to be clothed with our heavenly dwelling, because when we are clothed, we will not be found naked. For while we are in this tent, we groan and are burdened, because we do not wish to be unclothed but to be clothed with our heavenly dwelling. . . .
>
> *2 Corinthians 5:1–4*

The general consensus seems to be, as John Gilmore has expressed it, that "during the interval we are in conscious existence, although we are not yet in our resurrection bodies. We are not floating around in space as invisible spirits, without the capacity for speech or action. Neither are we asleep or unconscious in a temporary or lethargic state. We are to be very much alive and very near to Christ, for to be 'absent from the body' means 'to be present with the Lord.' "[16]

There are many things about this subject that we do not and cannot know for certain. But we do know with assurance that at death the souls of believers go immediately to heaven, where they are completely and utterly happy. And yet there is more and better to follow. As someone once put it, the moment we take the last breath on earth, we take our first breath in heaven. It was so with the dying thief, for did not our Lord say to him, "*today* you will be with me in paradise"?

After the thief voiced his request, "Jesus, remember me when you come into your kingdom" (Luke 23:42), the Lord's reply did much to answer our question. We must not read too much into the words of the thief, for he would have been very innocent of theology. However, in them there is an incipient acknowledgment of His royalty.

The thief's apprehension of who Christ is was doubtless very limited, but the Holy Spirit had been working in his heart in answer to the Savior's prayer, and in his heart was the germ of faith that drew forth the Master's pregnant words.

It should be noted that Jesus, as He sometimes does, did not answer the precise words of the man's petition but did something infinitely greater. He granted the desire of his heart. The thief did not and could not know that the exact words of his petition would not be fulfilled for at least two thousand years, until Christ enters fully into His kingdom.

Dr. Anderson Berry sees a designed correspondence between the thief's petition and the Lord's response:

> And he said to Jesus
> *And Jesus said to him*
> Lord,
> *I tell you the truth*
> Remember me
> *You shall be with me*
> When you come
> *Today*
> Into your Kingdom
> *In Paradise*

To the thief Jesus promised that to be absent from the body was to be immediately with the Lord.

We may draw three inferences from His reply:
1. That the soul survives the disintegration of the body.
2. That soul and body exist separately. While the body is still in the grave, the soul can be with Christ. The body of the thief would be disposed of roughly, but his soul would be in the immediate presence of Christ, in the place of departed spirits—paradise. His experience was not to be unconscious sleep, but conscious union with Christ.
3. That there is no gap between the moment of death and the entry of the redeemed soul into the joy and bliss of eternity.

This raises another question:
In the intermediate state, does the soul sleep?

It is contended by some religious groups that between death and the resurrection (a time usually termed "the intermediate state"), the soul "sleeps" —that is, exists in an unconscious state, a dreamless sleep. This phenomenon is known as "soul sleep." Its advocates maintain that Christ's assurance to the penitent thief allows another interpretation than that given above. As there is no punctuation in Luke's original Greek, it had to be supplied by the English translator, taking the context into account. The contention of those who defend "soul sleep" is that what Jesus really said was "I tell you the truth *today*, you will be with me in paradise," and *not*, "I tell you the truth, *today* you will be with me in paradise." So in their view, "today" here refers to the time Jesus was making the promise, not the time the thief would arrive in paradise.

But why should the Lord pinpoint the time at which He was speaking? The only reasonable meaning is the other option, that the soul of the thief would that very day be with Him in paradise.

It is true that death in Scripture is at times referred to as "sleep" (for example, John 11:11; 1 Cor. 15:6, 18, 20, 51; 1 Thess. 4:13–15). But in these passages, *sleep* is simply a euphemism for death and is not to be taken literally. The context makes that clear. Jesus used the word in that sense when He told the disciples that Lazarus had "fallen asleep." They took His words literally and responded, "Lord, if he sleeps, he will get better." Then Jesus told them plainly, "Lazarus is dead" (John 11:11–14).

There is no passage in Scripture that affirms that the soul sleeps. It is the *person* who sleeps, not the soul. The great problem that proponents of the "soul sleep" theory have never been able to solve convincingly is how to interpret several passages of Scripture that teach plainly that there is personal and conscious existence between death and the resurrection. The parable of Dives and Lazarus is one of these (Luke 16:19–31).

It is objected that Jesus did not give this parable or incident to afford insight into an intermediate state, but rather as a warning on the issues of life in our own earthly existence. While conceding that this may be true, does it necessarily exhaust all that He intended to teach? And is He at the same time likely to mislead us in the matter of the intermediate state? He obviously intended us to learn that both Dives and Lazarus were alive and conscious, or the parable would have no point at all.

Further, how can the concept of "soul sleep" be harmonized with the following Scriptures? "I say to you that many will come from the east and the west, and will take their places at the feast with Abraham, Isaac and Jacob in the kingdom of heaven" (Matt. 8:11). How could people sit down at a feast with the three patriarchs if they were asleep?

"Father Abraham, have pity on me and send Lazarus to dip the tip of his finger in water and cool my tongue, because I am in agony in this fire" (Luke 16:24). How could the rich man be in conscious torment if he was asleep?

"For me to live is Christ and to die is gain" (Phil. 1:21). In what way would it be gain to Paul if death brought only unconsciousness?

None of the great creeds of the church include "soul sleep" as an acceptable doctrine. However, Article Forty of the Forty-two Articles promulgated in the reign of Edward VI says:

> The souls of them that depart this life, do neither die with the bodies nor sleep idly. They which say that the souls of such as depart hence do sleep, being without all sense, feeling or perceiving, until the day of judgment . . . do utterly dissent from the right belief declared to us in Holy Scripture.

Is there such a place as purgatory?

"But now he has appeared once for all at the end of the ages to do away with sin by the sacrifice of himself."

Hebrews 9:26

A consideration of heaven without taking into account a dogma held by millions—that is, purgatory

—would be very incomplete. This dogma, promulgated by the Roman Catholic Church, has been summarized by one of their cardinals, J. Gibbons, in *Faith of Our Fathers* in the following terms:

> The Catholic church teaches that, besides a place of eternal torments for the wicked and of everlasting rest for the righteous, there exists in the next life a middle state of temporary punishment, allotted for those who have died in venial sin, or who have not satisfied the justice of God for sins already forgiven. She also teaches us that, although the souls confined to the intermediate state, commonly called purgatory, cannot help themselves, they may be aided by the suffrages of the faithful on earth.

Thus, Rome teaches that purgatory is "the place where the souls of by far the majority of deceased believers suffer anguish and are thereby gradually purified."

One would surely expect that for such a solemn prospect there would be a formidable array of Scripture passages to support it. But is this the case? In *The Catholic Dictionary* we read: "We would appeal to those general principles of Scripture, rather than to particular texts often alleged in proof of purgatory. *We doubt if they contain an explicit and direct reference to it.*"

Is *heaven* mentioned in Scripture? Many times. And *hell*? Many times. And *purgatory*? NOT ONCE. Nor was the idea introduced until the second century. And it was not decreed as an article of faith of the Roman Catholic Church until 1439 at the Council of Florence.

Does it not seem strange that the Scriptures are silent about it, the early church knew nothing of it, and fourteen centuries elapsed before even the Roman church officially adopted this coffer-filling belief? Little wonder that Hugh Latimer termed it "Pick-purse Purgatory."

Most Protestants do not fully realize that, according to this doctrine, even the devout and faithful members of the Roman church, except in rare cases (and even then no one can be sure), must experience the purgatorial fires, "the pains of which are more grievous than all the pains of this world" (St. Thomas Aquinas). The truly saintly Father F. W. Faber, who has given us many beautiful hymns, describes it thus:

> In pain beyond all earthly pains,
>   Favourites of Jesus, there they lie,
> Letting the fire burn out their stains
>   And worshipping God's purity.

Is this the way God treats His favorites? Is this the promised rest, the prepared place? Is this the prospect Paul had in view when he had such a desire to depart and be with Christ, which, he maintained, was "better by far" (Phil. 1:23)?

Because of purgatory, even the devout Catholic lives in fear of death and what might lie beyond. But Christ partook of our humanity for the express purpose of delivering "those who all their lives were held in slavery by their fear of death" (Heb. 2:15). The dogma of purgatory gives the Roman Catholic Church a stranglehold on its adherents in death as in life. *But there is not one shred of biblical evidence for it.*

"Purgation? Yes. Purgatory? No." So writes John Gilmore.

> Purgation does not require purgatory. Another way of putting it is to say purgatory is required but is past. . . . The Bible tells where purgatory *was*—The place was Calvary where Jesus died for our sins. He became our purgatory and took our hell. Hebrews 1:3 (NEB) says: "When he had brought about the *purgation* of sins, he took his seat at the right hand of Majesty on high." [17]

So with complete confidence in an inspired and infallible Bible, conscious as we are of having sinned deeply, we confess our sins to Christ, our one and only Mediator, and commit our souls to His keeping, in the sure and certain confidence that He is faithful to His promise and has cleansed us in the true purgatory of His own blood "which cleanses us from all sin."

What of infants and the mentally retarded?

"Jesus said, 'Let the little children come to me, and do not hinder them, for the kingdom of heaven belongs to such as these.' "

Matthew 19:14

> Note: In this section the term *infants* is intended to include all who die before reaching the years of moral accountability, as well as the mentally retarded.

This is a question that inevitably occurs when considering heaven, especially to parents who lose a little child or who have an older but mentally retarded child. Such children form a significant segment of the population of the whole world. What is their status?

"We believe that all dying in infancy are included in the election of grace and are regenerated and saved by Christ through the Spirit who works when and how he pleases." This statement of the Confession of Faith of the Christian Reformed Church is one with which most Christians would feel sympathy. The crucial question is, can it be supported from Scripture?

Two significant affirmations of Paul would, on the face of them, seem to include those who die before the age of moral accountability or are mentally retarded: "all have sinned and fall short of the glory of God," and "death reigned from the time of Adam to the time of Moses, even over those who did not sin by breaking a command, as did Adam" (Rom. 3:23; 5:14).

The Roman Catholic view that unbaptized infants are lost is repugnant to the Protestant Christian conscience, as well as being without a biblical basis. Romans 5:14,19 affirms that the whole race was involved in Adam's sin and its baleful consequences and that each person has inherited a corrupt nature, with consequent guilt and condemnation. But Millard Erickson offers this elaboration:

> As to guilt, just as with the imputation of righteousness, there must be some conscious and voluntary decision on our part. Until this is true, there is only a conditional imputation of guilt. Therefore no condemnation attaches until one reaches the age of responsibility. If a child dies before it is capable of making genuine moral decisions, the experience is the same. [18]

Most will agree that if there is salvation for infants, it will be through the operation of the grace of God and on the ground of the merits of Christ, not on the grounds of the merit or innocence of the infant. Clearly, those who have not attained years of responsibility have not sinned in a way similar to those who are adult. They have not deliberately rejected the gospel. As someone has put it: "As without sinful act of theirs, infants inherited corruption from Adam, so without personal act of theirs, salvation is provided for them in Christ." If this be so, it can be only because God credits their sin to Christ.

Scripture differentiates between those who are morally responsible for their actions and those who are not. The latter were expressly excluded by the Lord from the judgment that overtook the Israelites who refused to enter Canaan. "And little ones that you said would be taken captive, your children *who do not yet know good from bad*—they will enter the land" (Deut. 1:39). God also demonstrated concern for the "more than a hundred and twenty thousand people *who cannot tell their right hand from their left*" in pagan Nineveh (Jonah 4:11).

Jesus loved little children and often spoke about them. But *not once did He either say or imply that infants were in danger of being lost*. Indeed, His statements seemed to imply the very opposite, as the following passages will corroborate:

> Let the little children come to me . . . for the kingdom of heaven belongs to such as these.
> *Matthew 19:14*

> See that you do not look down on one of these little ones. For I tell you that their angels in heaven always see the face of my Father in heaven.
> *Matthew 18:10*

In the same way your Father in heaven is not willing that any of these little ones should be lost.

Matthew 18:14

I tell you the truth, unless you change and become like little children, you will never enter the kingdom of heaven.

Matthew 18:3

With reference to these Scriptures, Dr. A. H. Strong had this to say:

While these words seem intended to exclude all idea that infants are saved by their natural holiness or without the application of the blessings of the atonement, they also seem to include infants among the number of those who have a right to those blessings; in other words Christ's concern and care go so far as to choose infants to eternal life and to make them subjects of the Kingdom of heaven. [19]

From the above Scriptures, one can infer with confidence that, since Christ received infants here, He will not reject them there. On the contrary, was He not holding them up as examples of the type of person who would inherit the kingdom?

And hark! amid the sacred songs
Those heavenly voices raise,
Ten thousand thousand infant tongues
Unite in perfect praise.

Charles Wesley

The striking difference in David's grief over the death of his two sons—one an adult and the other an infant—affords evidence that even under the old covenant he was assured of infant salvation. Compare David's two laments:

> O my son Absalom! My son, my son Absalom! If only I had died instead of you—O Absalom, my son, my son!
>
> *2 Samuel 18:33*

> While the child was still alive, I fasted and wept. . . . But now that he is dead, why should I fast? Can I bring him back again? I will go to him, but he will not return to me.
>
> *2 Samuel 12:22–23*

A question that arises naturally when this subject is being discussed is, "What is the age of moral responsibility or accountability?" There can be no fixed age, because children do not mature at any fixed age. One suggested guideline is, "When they as an act of independent choice adopt, or reject the beliefs of their family or group, accept responsibility for that, and are sufficiently autonomous to do so, then they exclude themselves from God's gracious provision for their previous spiritual helplessness." [20]

We can rest in the fact that "the Lord knows those who are His" (2 Tim. 2:19).

With this body of Scripture under our feet, together with an enlightened evangelical conscience, we need have no hesitation in believing that our little ones are "safe in the arms of Jesus." In addition, we can say with confidence, "Will not the Judge of all the earth do right?" (Gen. 18:25).

THREE

Changes and Progress in Heaven

What will heaven be like?
Will mansions be awaiting us?
What changes will there be?
Will there be development and progress in heaven?
What is the role of angels in heaven?

Some people talk about heaven as they would about an imaginary place. They do it with tongue in cheek and a knowing smile, as if to say heaven is a human invention, a never-never land, a realm of dreams, and not to be taken seriously.

Others say heaven is a benevolent state of mind, a vague vacuum, or a reward for being good. Some say heaven or hell is what you make of this life—a projection of the best in yourself.

... But heaven as a place? Never! [21]

Charles F. Ball

Responsibility for these angelic beings is "to minister to them who shall be heirs of salvation." Although they are unable experientially to fathom the redemptive grace of God (1 Peter 1:12), their assignment of ministry to the heirs of salvation is varied. In addition to the heralding tasks associated with the birth of Jesus, angels strengthened him in Gethsemane (Luke 22:43), stood sentinel at the empty tomb to announce the Lord's resurrection, and gently chided the disciples for seeking the living among the dead. [22]

Paige Patterson

What will heaven be like?

"No eye has seen, no ear has heard, no mind has conceived what God has prepared for those who love him. . . ."

1 Corinthians 2:9

The popular view of heaven is that if such an abode really exists, it will be a place of physical pleasure and luxury—a place where all unpleasant experiences are excluded and every aesthetic desire gratified. It is usually conceived in earthly and material terms—only better.

The Westminster Catechism has as its first question, "What is the chief end of man?" And the correct answer: "The chief end of man is to glorify God and enjoy Him forever." The modern equivalent, however, appears to be, "The chief end of God is to gratify man." This outlook is carried over into the popular view of heaven, but the necessary conditions on which entry into heaven is granted are given scant consideration.

Embedded in the cultures of most primitive peoples is some expectation of life after death. Generally, the need to appease a supreme spirit and other hostile spirits is present, as also is the element of retribution. This in turn engenders fear, which is endemic in most non-Christian cultures. In some belief systems, there is also the concept of reward for well-doing.

Buddhists and Hindus have their *nirvana*, which promises the bliss of being absorbed into the supreme spirit. Native North Americans have their eternal hunting grounds, and Muslims, their palaces of sensual delights. This universal and intuitive belief that persists throughout the world among widely diverse and scattered races must surely have some corresponding reality, distorted though it may be by various religions. Man's intuitions and cravings surely do not mock him.

Belief in a life hereafter was also a tenet of the Jewish faith in Old and New Testament days. Its distinctive view of heaven was *sheol*, the Old Testament name for the place of departed souls. The corresponding New Testament word is *hades*. "Sheol often means the place or state of the soul between death and resurrection when the soul will be joined with a spiritual body. The clearest indication of different conditions in Sheol is in our Lord's parable in Luke 16:19–31, where the rich man is pictured as in torment, while Lazarus was in Abraham's bosom," [23] a figure of speech for heaven.

In early Jewish thought, sheol was not primarily a place of retribution and reward, although those elements were not absent. To Jews it was supremely the place where their ancestors lay. Hence the oft-repeated expression, "they were gathered to their fathers."

But the godly Jews entertained more exalted expectations, which were voiced by prophet and psalmist. Here are some samples:

I know that my Redeemer lives, and that in the end he will stand upon the earth. . . . in my flesh I will see God;

I myself will see him with my own eyes—I, and not another.

Job 19:25–27

And I—in righteousness I will see your face; when I awake, I will be satisfied with seeing your likeness.

Psalm 17:15

You guide me with your counsel, and afterward you will take me into glory. Whom have I in heaven but you? And earth has nothing I desire besides you.

Psalm 73:24–25

Yet the Christian concept of heaven far outstrips even Jewish thought. It is immeasurably higher and nobler than Old Testament speculations. As Alexander Maclaren put it, heaven is a place of indescribable splendor, of blessedness and peace. We are left by its biblical description with an image of a life that will far transcend anything we have known hitherto. So incredibly glorious is it, that we are compelled to express it in negations and by symbols of grandeur and majesty, "gathered," as Maclaren said, "from what is noblest and best in human building and society."

But what makes heaven heaven for the Christian is the perpetual presence of God as Sovereign Ruler of the universe, and yet at the same time as our loving heavenly Father, and the reality of enjoying forever the companionship of our Redeemer and Lord.

Now the dwelling of God is with men, and he will live with them. They will be his people, and God himself will be with them and be their God.

Revelation 21:3

Will mansions be awaiting us?

"In my Father's house *are many mansions*: if it were not so, I would have told you. I go to prepare a place for you. And if I go and prepare a place for you, I will come again, and receive you unto myself; that where I am, there ye may be also."

John 14:2–3 KJV

These treasured words have imparted more comfort to dying saints and grieving relatives than any other portion of Scripture. Scottish writer Ian Maclaren bore this testimony: "Whenever I am called to a house of sickness or sorrow, *I always read to the troubled folk John 14.* Nothing else is so effective. If a man is sinking into unconsciousness, and you read about many mansions, he will come back and whisper 'mansions,' and will wait until you finish—'that where I am, there you may be also.' " Maclaren lived in a day when people were familiar with the Scriptures, but today not all would recognize the allusion.

"Trust me!" our Lord urged His followers. He spoke these words on the night before the cross to His dearly loved disciples, who were devastated at the thought of His leaving them. So He encouraged them to keep on trusting Him.

'Twas the Master himself who said it
    To the sorrowful little band,
Facing an hour of darkness
    That they could not understand.

The light of their lives was fading,
    Their eyes with tears were dim,
The rugged men were shaken
    At the thought of losing Him.

"Let not your heart be troubled!"
　　Never was voice so sweet,
　Never was look more kindly
　　Nor assurance more complete.

"Let not your heart be troubled!"
　　You believe in God most High?
　And one with God the Father,
　　Equal with Him am I.

We have every reason not to let our hearts be troubled. "What was the earthly paradise of Eden compared to that purchased by the Last Adam?" asked Nevins. "The price it cost to the Purchaser everyone knows. Having purchased it, he is gone to prepare it and set it in order, and lay out his skill on it. O what a place Jesus will make of it!"

However, the translator's use of the word *mansions* in the King James Version has given rise in some minds to a concept the word was never intended to convey. *Mansions*, as used today, conjures up the picture of a majestic earthly mansion and has inspired many hymns, such as:

A tent or cottage, why should I care?
They're building a palace for me over there;
Though exiled from home, yet still I may sing;
All glory to God, I'm a child of the King.

Harriett E. Buell

But that was not at all the meaning of the word when Jesus used it. The word appears only infrequently in Scripture, and in John 14:23 the original Greek is translated "abode" in the King James Version and "home" in the New International Version. It is a neutral word and carries no illusions of grandeur, but just means a "dwelling place." Its classical use is a "stopping place on a journey."

This clarification may spoil many a good sermon, but understanding the real meaning of the word more than compensates for any supposed loss, because Jesus added, "we will come to him and make our home with him" (v. 23). A home indwelt by the Trinity is no ordinary place! Jesus assured us that the homes in heaven are permanent dwelling-places, not makeshift shacks. There will be no substandard housing in heaven.

In this paragraph, the Lord was further assuring his emotionally disturbed disciples that the parting would be only temporary. And He promised a joyous reunion, saying in effect, "If I go, I will return. Don't be cast down!" He told them that in His Father's house there are "*many* rooms." No disciple need fear exclusion, there would be ample room for all.

Alexander Maclaren points out that in the expression "my Father's house," there is a blending of two ideas—domestic familiarity and the reality of which the temple was a symbol. The temple also had many rooms, porches, and courts for the thronging crowds. [24]

Another familiar picture assures us that heaven will be no ordinary place. Believers constitute the bride of Christ, and of them Jesus said, "I no longer call you servants. . . . Instead, I have called you friends" (John 15:15). This happy relationship ensures that we will not be housed in servants' quarters, but in a bridal suite.

The disciples were apparently confused as to what His departure meant, so the Lord explained to them, in effect: "You trust in God? Trust also in me. In our past relationship, have I ever broken my word to you? If my departure were not in your best interests, would I not have told you? Trust me!"

When Dr. R. W. Dale, the great preacher, lay dying, a great horror of darkness came over him, and the one who had established the faith of thousands found his own faith failing him. Happily, he lived long enough to conquer and to tell the story of his victory. Here is his account:

> The house was quiet. Soon after midnight I awoke in great pain, and a terrible distress came over me. I was full of fear. I did not wish to disturb my wife and daughters; they were worn out with anxious watching. So I lay silently, struggling against the indescribable terror of an unknown dread. When the conflict reached its worst, it seemed as tho' Christ Himself came, and standing close beside me said, "Let not your heart be troubled. You believe God, believe me also," etc. That steadied me, and I felt safe and strong in the arms of Christ. [25]

Heaven as home

One reason why John 14:2–3 is such a popular passage is that it pictures heaven as a home. *Home* means different things to different people. To the homeless it remains a tantalizing mirage, an unattainable ideal. To others it conjures up memories of strife, abuse, and absence of love. But to those more fortunate, home is a place "where longings draw, and around which happy memories cluster."

> I know not, O I know not
> What social joys are there;

> What radiancy of glory,
>> What bliss beyond compare.

F. W. Faber

Ideally, home is a place where loving and caring parents provide for their children all that they need, where they train and discipline them lovingly and firmly, and where family members enjoy uninhibited fellowship and fun—a place of love, understanding, and security, where sorrows are jointly shared. There is a saying in Africa, "Only mention home to the weary traveler, and his legs become as bars of iron."

> As when the weary traveller gains
>> The top of some o'er looking hill
> His heart revives if o'er the plains
>> He sees his home, tho' distant still.

But there are some who will barely make it home. Paul speaks of one such: "he himself will be saved, but only as one escaping through the flames" (1 Cor. 3:15).

> Safe home! safe home in port!
>> Rent cordage, shattered deck,
> Torn sails, provisions short,
>> And only not a wreck.
> But, O! the joy upon the shore,
> To tell the voyage perils o'er.

St. Joseph of the Stadium

How much better to have an abundant entrance.

What changes will there be?
". . . the first heaven and the first earth had passed away, and there was no longer any sea. . . .

"I did not see a temple in the city. . . . The city does not need the sun or the moon to shine on it. . . ."
Revelation 21:1, 22, 23

It appears that in heaven we will be independent of much that we deem absolutely essential and indispensable now. For example, there is no night there. Imagine a week without sleep! What a boon night is when we are bone weary. But, since heaven is "better by far" than life here on earth, there must be blessing in the seemingly negative characteristics included in the book of Revelation.

Let us consider some of these beneficial absences.

1. *No Temple.* "I did not see a temple in the city" (21:22).

To a Jew, this would be as inconceivable as a city without a church would be to us. The beautiful temple was the outstanding feature and glory of the earthly Jerusalem. Its citizens took great pride in it. Matthew records, "Jesus left the temple and was walking away when his disciples came up to him to call his attention to its buildings" (24:1). The temple was to them the visible symbol of God dwelling in their midst, for God Himself had said to Moses, "Then have them make a sanctuary for me, and I will dwell among them" (Ex. 25:8).

In heaven, however, there is no longer any need for a special building set apart for the worship of God, for God is Himself the temple. The earthly temple is replaced by the *immediate presence* of the omnipresent God. So we can bid farewell to troublesome building funds and denominational differences and "worship Him in spirit and truth!"

Father of Jesus, love's reward,
What rapture will it be
Prostrate before Thy throne to lie,
And gaze and gaze on Thee.

F. W. Faber

2. *No Sea.* "... there was no longer any sea" (21:1).

A sealess heaven! This seems almost as impossible as a world with no night. The sea fills such an enormous role in our life on earth that we can scarcely conceive its absence. But there would be benefits. Storm and shipwreck would be a thing of the past. To the exile or emigrant, the sea means separation from home and loved ones, and the severing of cherished friendships. As he wrote of his vision of heaven, John was himself experiencing the loneliness of an exile on the Patmos Isle.

The restless, never-ceasing surge of the sea aptly symbolizes the uncertainty and unwelcome changes of life. So a sealess heaven would convey to John's readers the idea that there will be no more exile or separation, no more sundered friendships, no more loneliness, rather, reunion with loved ones.

Instead of the sea, there is a beautiful river flowing from the throne of God and of the Lamb down the great street of the city of God. On each side of the river there grows the tree of life, which yields its fruit every month (22:2). Instead of the evils of the sea, heaven holds a life-giving, fruit-producing river. The reader will have no problem in interpreting the symbolism.

3. *No Death.* "There will be no more death" (21:4).

What comfort and reassurance these six words convey to the troubled heart. The king of terrors, the last enemy, will never be able to breach the pearly gates and disturb the bliss of heaven! No more death-bed vigils or funerals. The hearse will have made its last journey.

4. *No Mourning and Crying.* "There will be no . . . mourning or crying" (21:4).

Mourning and crying caused by the poignancy of bereavement or the ravages of sin will be no more. Sooner or later the trauma of bereavement overtakes us all on this earth. In marriage, one partner must usually traverse that experience, with its accompanying period of grief and loss. Most of us must face the loss of parents. Christians feel these things just as deeply as others; we are not dehumanized by our convictions about the future. But we do have the benefit of the compensatory comfort of God and the sure hope of resurrection.

5. *No Pain.* "There will be no more . . . pain, for the old order of things has passed away" (21:4).

No more cruel traffic accidents with their painful aftermath. No more arthritis. With the increase of years one must face the wasting and disintegration of the body and the pain and weakness that often accompany the process. Indeed, at any stage of life we are liable to experience pain in varying degrees. All of this is absent from heaven.

6. *No Hunger or Thirst.* "Never again will they hunger; never again will they thirst" (7:16).

Two of the most agonizing experiences people can suffer will be banished. Think of what this will mean to the starving millions of Africa and India who have forgotten what it is like to have a full stomach! No one in heaven will ever again feel the pangs of hunger or the agony of thirst.

7. *No Tears.* "He will wipe every tear from their eyes" (21:4).

"I do not know what handkerchief the Lord will use," said Charles H. Spurgeon, "but I know that He will wipe away *all tears* from the face of every citizen of heaven." All tears—those arising from our own sin and failure, or from sorrow or bereavement, or those caused by others. Because there will be no more crying, there will be no more tears, or the occasion for them. On earth, tears will flow again, but in heaven the Comforter will give permanent consolation.

8. *No Night.* "There will be no more night" (22:5).

After a long and tiring day, how welcome are the shades of night—one of God's choicest blessings. Our weary bodies need the rest of night to recruit strength for the demands of the new day. Surely the absence of night would be a great calamity, not a blessing. Then why is what is now a medium of refreshment and renewal banished from heaven?

There is a good reason. Our changed bodies will no longer be in need of the recuperative process of sleep. True, there will be abundant activity in heaven, but it will be *without fatigue or exhaustion,* for our bodies will be like His. "And we eagerly await a Savior from there, the Lord Jesus Christ, who . . . *will transform our lowly bodies so that they will be like his glorious body*" (Phil. 3:21).

There are many senses in which night is beneficent, but Scripture discloses negative features as well, for darkness is symbolic of sin. "This is the verdict: Light has come into the world, but men loved darkness instead of light because their deeds were evil" (John 3:19).

Night is associated with dark and evil crimes. Sorrow seems more poignant during the night, and pain more acute. But heaven introduces a new order. Instead of the dark night of anxiety and fear, there is only the light beaming from the face of Jesus Christ (2 Cor. 4:6).

> No night shall be in heaven! no gathering gloom
> Shall o'er that glorious landscape ever come;
> No tears shall fall in sadness o'er those flowers
> That breathe their fragrance through celestial hours.
>
> No night in heaven! but endless noon;
> No fast declining sun, nor waning moon:
> But there the Lamb shall yield perpetual light,
> 'Mid pastures green and waters ever bright.
>
> No night shall be in heaven! O, had I faith
> To rest in what the faithful witness saith,
> That faith should make these hideous phantoms flee,
> And leave no night on earth to me.

9. *No Sun or Moon.* "The city does not need the sun or the moon to shine on it, for the glory of God gives it light, and the Lamb is its lamp" (21:23).

Heaven is bathed in the eternal brilliance that proceeds from Him who described Himself as the Light of the World. There will be no need for external, man-made lamps. To all eternity He is the light-bearer, from whose face radiates the light of the glory of God. The beneficent ministry of sun and moon is superseded by the perpetual illumination of the Sun of Righteousness.

> No need of sun or moon in that day
> Which never is followed by night,

> Where Jesus' beauties display
>   A pure and permanent light.
>
> The Lamb is their light and their sun,
>   And lo, by reflection they shine,
> With Jesus ineffably one,
>   And bright with effulgence divine.
>
> *Charles Wesley*

10. *No Shut Gates.* "On no day will its gates ever be shut" (21:25).

Because all that is evil and unclean is excluded from the heavenly city, security measures will no longer be needed. There will be open access yet perfect security. Then Isaiah's prophecy will be fulfilled: "Your gates will always stand open, they will never be shut, day or night" (60:11).

Will there be development and progress in heaven?

"Now we see but a poor reflection as in a mirror; then we shall see face to face. Now I know in part; then I shall know fully, even as I am fully known."

1 Corinthians 13:12

Opinion is divided sharply on this subject, and so one can speak only tentatively and present one's personal view. One reason for this division of viewpoint is that there is no clear-cut scriptural statement that there will be advance and development in heaven. But from what is said, it is possible to draw reasonable inferences.

One protagonist says, "It will be a life of growth without limit." And another, "We will not grow in heaven." One thing is blessedly certain; we will not advance in sinlessness, for we will be like the Sinless One (1 John 3:2).

The question may be raised, if heaven is a state of perfection, does this mean that in one tremendous experience we attain a static state, beyond which there can be no progress or growth?

When Paul says that after knowledge, prophecy, and tongues have passed away, faith, *hope*, and love remain, does that not imply that growth and advance is possible in heaven? Will our knowledge of God ever reach the point where we exhaust His wisdom? (1 Cor. 13:8, 13).

What is hope but the anticipation of positive and joyous experiences in the future? If heaven means that we reach a static state of perfection, does that not deprive "hope" of any real meaning? In this connection W. Graham Scroggie writes helpfully:

> Christian hope is holy expectation, and there will never come a time when that hope will die, for were that possible, much of heaven would go. But in our progress there, new vistas of wonder will ever be opening up, new glories of our inheritance will for ever be revealed, new heights of attainment ever be disclosed. [26]

Scripture encourages us to expect that in heaven every hope and holy expectation will find fulfillment, and yet hope will abide. Hope for what? Is it not true that our perfect Lord "grew in wisdom and stature, and in favor with God and men" although He was perfect? (Luke 2:52).

Life in heaven will be perfect, but it will be a relative perfection as of a child in relation to a parent: perfect, yet not yet fully perfect—still capable of further growth and development. The Greek word for *perfect* is rendered *mature* in many recent translations, and this suggests the possibility of growth.

In an article called "Reunion in Heaven," Sir W. Robertson Nicoll wrote, "The eternal life of the redeemed will never reach a point where no advance is possible." Does not the assertion that we shall know as we are known imply that our capacity for knowledge will be expanded? How can one think without growing in knowledge?

Would a heaven without change be an alluring prospect? In his *Christian Theology*, Millard Erickson advances an alternative view. He maintains, "the stable situation in heaven is not a fixed state short of one's goal, but a state of completion beyond which there can be no advance. Reaching the goal will bring perfect satisfaction, therefore we will not grow in heaven. We will however exercise the perfect character received from God." [27]

But surely progress in love and joy is not inconsistent with perfection, if it is recognized that ours is only a relative perfection. While this cannot be proved categorically, it is a reasonable inference. Could there not be degrees of growth within perfection?

Abraham Kuyper, the noted Dutch theologian, expresses his conviction that there will be room for growth in heaven:

> The complete sanctification of my personality, body and soul, does not imply that my holy disposition is now in contact with all the fulness of the divine resources. On the contrary, as I ascend from glory to glory, I shall find in the infinite depths of the divine Being, the eternal object of richest delight in ever-increasing measure.

Because the love of God is infinite and therefore surpasses human knowledge, does it not follow that if we could exhaust that knowledge, we would be God? For only God can fully know God. In heaven we will be perfected to the height of our capacity. Alexander Maclaren illustrates this concept from the heavenly bodies. In the heavens some planets roll nearer the sun, others further out, yet each keeps to its course. All those saved will have a perfection like that of Christ when they see Him, but all will grow increasingly like Him throughout eternity.

We have seen from that in the Father's house there are many "rest stops" along the highway, where travelers may pause on the journey. So the two concepts of rest and progress are combined in this picture. While we will not be growing *toward* perfection, we will be growing *in* perfection. [28]

What is the role of angels in heaven?

". . . when God brings his firstborn into the world, he says, 'Let all God's angels worship him.' In speaking of the angels he says, 'He makes his angels winds, his servants flames of fire.' "

Hebrews 1:6–7

An angel is defined as an attendant or messenger of God. The presence and ministry of angels on earth and in heaven is mentioned no fewer than three hundred times in the Bible, which is the only authentic source of information about them. But in spite of this frequent mention, they receive only minimal attention in the contemporary world, both secular and religious. This has caused them to be referred to as the most ignored personalities of Scripture.

Three attitudes toward angels prevail among those to whom the Scriptures are not the final authority. (1) The existence of angels is acknowledged as an article of faith, but further than that, little interest is taken in their role. (2) Accounts of the activity of angels are taken as figures of speech, conveying the idea of heavenly messages or of divine influence. (3) The subject is dismissed cavalierly as having no basis in fact—mere fantasy.

In the demythologizing of Scripture that he espoused, Rudolf Bultmann, while noting the prominent role ascribed to angels in the New Testament, asserted,

> Today we no longer believe in such spiritual beings. We now understand through our increased knowledge of nature, that disease is not caused by demons, but by viruses and bacteria. . . . It is impossible to use electric lights and the wireless and to avail ourselves of modern medical and surgical discoveries and at the same time believe in the New Testament world of spirits and miracles. [29]

A similar rationalistic attitude toward angels was encountered both by Jesus and by Paul, for "The Sadducees say that there is no resurrection, and that there are neither angels nor spirits" (Acts 23:8). The Pharisees were not party to this denial, but in our day the church at large seems almost to have dropped the subject from thought and teaching. It was not always so in the church.

In his *Paradise Lost*, John Milton, the blind poet, had Adam saying these words:

> Nor think though men were none,
> That heaven would want spectators,
> God want praise.

> Millions of spirit creatures walk the earth
> Unseen both when we walk and when we sleep,
> All these with ceaseless praise His works behold,
>   Both day and night.

What are angels like?

The standard conception of their appearance as given in the Oxford dictionary is, "Usually shown in pictures as a being in human form with wings, dressed in long, white robes."

From the Bible we learn that they are immaterial, spiritual beings, although at times they assume human form. They are represented as God's entourage, constantly at His service. Seraphim and cherubim are portrayed as winged (Isa. 6:2), but it is not stated that all angels have wings, although they may.

Because in appearance they are human-like, it has been easy for them to be mistaken for human beings. At times their glorious and shining appearance has aroused fear in the onlookers. Speaking of an angel, Matthew wrote, "His appearance was like lightning, and his clothes were white as snow. The guards were so afraid of him that they shook and became like dead men" (Matt. 28:3–4).

Angels appear to be numberless. Heaven is teeming with them. Jesus gave insight into their numbers at the time of His arrest in the Garden of Gethsemane: "Do you think I cannot call on my Father, and he will at once put at my disposal more than twelve legions of angels?" (Matt. 26:53).

When it is remembered that a Roman legion could comprise anything from three thousand to six thousand men, the angelic population is difficult to conceive. In Revelation 5:11 mention is made of the angels encircling the throne of God: "Then I looked and heard the voice of many angels, numbering thousands upon thousands, and ten thousand times ten thousand."

Though angels are glorious and holy personalities, yet they are but created beings who have access into the presence of God (Ps. 103:20). They are of high intelligence, but our divinely established relation to them comes as a surprise. To the Corinthian believers Paul asked a revealing question: "Do you not know that we will judge angels?" (1 Cor. 6:3). Jesus also revealed that they "neither marry nor [are] given in marriage" (Matt. 22:30).

What are their activities?

1. On many critical occasions they ministered *to the Lord*—at His birth, after the temptation in the desert, in Gethsemane, at the tomb of Joseph, and at the Ascension.

2. They have a special ministry *to believers* here on earth. "Are not all angels ministering spirits sent to serve those who will inherit salvation?" (Heb. 1:14). It would appear from this passage that in heaven we will be surprised when we discover how active angels have been on our behalf.

3. They have a special ministry *to children*. "See that you do not look down on one of these little ones. For I tell you that their angels in heaven always see the face of my Father in heaven" (Matt. 18:10).

4. They know about and rejoice over the salvation of the lost. "I tell you, there is rejoicing in the presence of the angels of God over one sinner who repents" (Luke 15:10).

5. At the Rapture, the angels will be the reapers. "The weeds are the sons of the evil one, and the enemy who sows them is the devil. The harvest is the end of the age, and the harvesters are angels" (Matt. 13:38–39).

To sum up,

- Angels worship and serve God.
- They minister to children and believers.
- They communicate God's messages to human beings.
- They execute judgment on God's enemies.
- They will be involved in the Second Advent.

FOUR

Rewards and Resurrection Bodies

Who will receive rewards?
What do the promised crowns signify?
What will our resurrection bodies be like?
What was our Lord's resurrection body like?
Will there be time in heaven?

Here is a searching word—the *motive* of our work is what counts. In that day God will test everything by His standard of truth, and if it meets with his approval, a reward will be given. The reward is not salvation, for salvation is of grace, altogether apart from works (Eph. 2:8–9). But this reward is for faithful service, because of salvation.

We will have bodies fit for the full life of God to indwell and express itself for ever. We will be able to eat but will not need to. We will be able to move rapidly through space and matter. We will be ageless and not know pain, tears, sorrow, sickness or death. We will have bodies of splendor. In a promise to the Old Testament saints, the Lord compared our glorious bodies to the shining of the moon and stars (Dan. 12:3). Christ's glorified body is described as shining like the sun in its strength.

Rene Pache[30]

Who will receive rewards?

"Blessed are you when men hate you, when they exclude you and insult you and reject your name as
evil, because of the Son of Man. Rejoice in that day
and leap for joy, because great is your reward in
heaven."

Luke 6:22–23

"The whole subject of rewards for the believer in
heaven is one that seems to be thought of only seldom by the ordinary Christian, or even by the aver-
age student of the Scriptures. It is at once both a
joyous and a solemn theme, and should serve as a potent incentive for holiness of life." So wrote Wilbur
M. Smith many years ago, and circumstances have
changed little since then with regard to this topic.

There are spiritual pedants who regard the
whole concept of rewards for service as a very sec-
ond-rate motivation. They liken it to offering candy
to a child if he will be good. But Jesus in no way offered support to this viewpoint. The verses at the
head of this chapter teach the reverse, as do many
other of His statements. The Apostle Paul also teaches about rewards in several of his letters.

It hardly need be said that no meritorious acts of
ours can win salvation, for that is a result of God's incredible and unmerited love. But the very fact that
Jesus spoke of rewards for service on a number of occasions would indicate that He considered their
granting an important article of faith. But in no way
did He suggest or imply that service was a method of
accumulating merit and thus receiving salvation.
Eternal life is a gift, not a reward.

The language in which the concept of rewards is clothed is highly symbolic and metaphorical and should be interpreted accordingly. Of course, faithful service brings rewards in *this* life as well as in the life to come. Both are mentioned in the following verse: " 'I tell you the truth,' Jesus said to them, 'no one who has left home or wife or brothers or parents or children for the sake of the kingdom of God will fail to receive many times as much *in this age and, in the age to come*, eternal life' " (Luke 18:29).

The New Testament *opens* with the Lord's promise of reward in the Beatitudes: "Blessed are you when people insult you, persecute you and falsely say all kinds of evil against you because of me. Rejoice and be glad, because *great is your reward* in heaven" (Matt. 5:11–12). This reward is for the person who endures slander and persecution *for the sake of the Lord*.

The New Testament *closes* with the Lord's assurance, "Behold, I am coming soon! *My reward is with me*, and I will give to everyone according to what he has done" (Rev. 22:12).

Since Jesus said that the reward for affliction borne for His sake is great and is a cause for rejoicing, we should take His words seriously and not dismiss them cavalierly as some do.

Paul is equally definite on this point: "For we must all appear before the judgment seat of Christ, that each one may receive what is due him for the things done while in the body, whether good or bad" (2 Cor. 5:10). From this passage we learn that our past deeds will confront us at the judgment seat, but it is equally clear that there *the salvation of the believer is not at issue.* That important matter was settled forever at the Cross, when our substitute graciously bore the judgment that was justly due to us for our sins. As a result of that blessed event, Paul assured believers, "Through him [Christ], *everyone who believes is justified from everything* you could not be justified from by the law of Moses" (Acts 13:39). The blessed consequence is that "Therefore there is now no condemnation for those who are in Christ Jesus" (Rom. 8:1).

So the believer need cherish no fear of losing eternal life at the judgment seat. But it might be objected, "Did not Paul have a fear of being a castaway?" When Paul wrote of that possibility, it was not because he was in fear of losing his salvation. The word *castaway*, as it is rendered in the King James Version of 1 Corinthians 9:27, is better rendered "disqualified." Paul was speaking in the context of competing in the Isthmian games. The fear he entertained was that, after having exhorted others how to run so as to win the coveted prize, he himself might be disqualified for the victor's crown. After all, eternal life is not a reward but a gift.

All true believers who stand before the judgment seat will qualify for heaven, but not all will receive the same reward. Someone once said, "Rewards will be calculated more on the basis of fidelity and suffering rather than on successful ventures." We are, however, strongly exhorted to "watch out that you do not lose what you have worked for, but that you may be rewarded fully" (2 John 8).

In the parables of the minas (Luke 19:11–27) and the talents (Matt. 25:14–30), Jesus taught that each believer has differing abilities and capacities. That is something over which we have no control and for which we are not responsible. The parable of the minas teaches that where there is equal ability but unequal faithfulness, there will be a smaller reward. On the other hand, the parable of the talents tells us that where there is unequal ability but equal faithfulness, the rewards will be the same. Christ's judgment and the reward bestowed will be according to the use we make of the opportunities given to us.

These parables, and indeed the whole subject of rewards for service, underline the importance of how we act here and now. It is now that we are determining our future status and reward in heaven.

> In hope of that immortal crown,
>   I now the cross sustain
> And gladly wander up and down,
>   And smile at toil and pain:
> I suffer out my three score years,
>   Till my Deliverer come,
> And wipe away His servant's tears,
>   And take His exile home.

Charles Wesley

What do the promised crowns signify?

"Now there is in store for me the crown of righteousness. . . ."

2 Timothy 4:8

The rewards promised in heaven are sometimes represented by the symbol of a crown. In the Greek culture a crown might be either an ornamental headdress worn by a king or queen or a wreath worn as a symbol of victory.

Before considering the significance of the crown awarded to victors, we should have a clear conception of the nature of heaven's rewards, for we are apt to equate them with our earthly reward system—equal pay for equal work. The idea of merit is thus involved. But a heavenly crown is not a matter of *quid pro quo*. In the heavenly rewards, merit is expressly excluded. Our Lord's word to His disciples makes this clear:

> Suppose one of you had a servant plowing or looking after the sheep. Would he say to the servant when he comes in from the field, "Come along now and sit down to eat"? Would he not rather say, "Prepare my supper, get yourself ready and wait on me while I eat and drink; after that you may eat and drink"? Would he thank the servant because he did what he was told to do? *So you also, when you have done everything you were told to do, should say, "We are unworthy servants; we have only done our duty."*
>
> Luke 17:7–10

Heaven's rewards are all a matter of God's grace. They are God's generous recognition of selfless and sacrificial service. G. Campbell Morgan goes so far as to assert that service for reward is not Christian, but un-Christian! "He emptied himself. He served 'for the joy set before him.' Yes, but what was that joy? The joy of lifting other people and blessing them." [31]

The fact that the laborer who was hired to work only at the eleventh hour received the same wage as the one who had worked all day underlies the fact that most of the wage he received was not earned, but was a generous gift from the master. When one of the full-time laborers charged his master with unfairness, he replied,

> Friend, I am not being unfair to you. Didn't you agree to work for a denarius? Take your pay and go. I want to give the man who was hired last the same as I gave you. Don't I have the right to do what I want with my own money? Or are you envious because I am generous?
>
> *Matthew 20:13–15*

We are not told precisely what form the crowns in heaven will take, but John Mac Arthur, Jr.'s view has much to commend it: "Believers' rewards aren't something you wear on your head like a crown. . . . Your reward in heaven will be your capacity for service in heaven. . . . Heaven's crowns are what we will experience, eternal life, eternal joy, eternal service and eternal blessedness." [32]

In the New Testament there are two Greek words translated "crown." One is *diadema*, a royal turban worn by Persian kings. It is always the symbol of kingly or imperial dignity. It refers to the kind of crown Jesus receives. The other word is *stephanos*, the victor's crown, "a symbol of triumph in the Olympic games or some such contest—hence by metonymy, a reward or prize" (Vine). It was a crown of leaves or vines, beautifully woven. This is the word that is used to denote the rewards of heaven.

Here are some of the crowns mentioned in Scripture.

1. *Crown of Life*

"Blessed is the man who perseveres under trial, because when he has stood the test, he will receive the *crown of life* that God has promised to those who love him."

James 1:12

"Be faithful, even to the point of death, and I will give you the *crown of life.* "

Revelation 2:10

This crown is bestowed in recognition of enduring and triumphing over trial and persecution even to the point of martyrdom. The motivation must be love for Christ.

2. Crown of Righteousness

"Now there is in store for me the *crown of righteousness,* which the Lord, the righteous Judge, will award to me on that day—and not only to me, but also to all who have longed for his appearing."

2 Timothy 4:8

This crown is awarded to those who have completed the Christian race with integrity, with eyes fixed on the coming Lord. It is the reward for fulfilling the ministry entrusted to one.

3. Incorruptible Crown

"They do it to get a *crown* that will not last; but we do it to get a *crown that will last forever.*"

1 Corinthians 9:25

This crown is won by those who strive for mastery, for excellence. Here Paul is using the figure of the pentathlon with its tremendous demand of physical stamina. The crown is awarded to the disciplined.

4. *Crown of Rejoicing*
"For what is our hope, or joy, or *crown of rejoicing*? Are not even ye in the presence of our Lord Jesus Christ at his coming?"

1 Thessalonians 2:19 KJV

This is the crown of the soul-winner. It will be cause for rejoicing when, in heaven, we meet those who have been won to Christ through our ministry. This crown is open to every believer.

5. *Crown of Glory*
"Be shepherds of God's flock that is under your care, serving as overseers—not because you must, but because you are willing, as God wants you to be. . . . And when the Chief Shepherd appears, you will receive the *crown of glory* that will never fade away."

1 Peter 5:2–4

This promised award for spiritual leaders in the church should provide strong motivation for sacrificial pastoral ministry.

However, none of these crowns is awarded automatically. There are qualifying conditions attached to each, and it is possible to forfeit a crown through unwatchfulness. In the letter to the church at Philadelphia, the risen Lord warned the believers: "I am coming soon. Hold on to what you have, *so that no one will take your crown*" (Rev. 3:11). This is a contemporary warning to us, as well, who are often surrounded by competing claims for our love and loyalty.

> 'Tis God's all-animating voice
> That calls thee from on high,

'Tis His own hand presents the prize
    To thine aspiring eye.

That prize with peerless glories bright,
    Which shall new lustre boast,
When victor's wreaths and monarch's gems
    Shall blend in common dust.

Blest Savior, introduced by Thee
    Have I my race begun;
And crowned with victory at Thy feet
    I'll lay my honors down.

Philip Doddridge

What will our resurrection bodies be like?

"But someone may ask, 'How are the dead raised? With what kind of body will they come?' How foolish! What you sow does not come to life unless it dies. When you sow, you do not plant the body that will be, but just a seed. . . . But God gives it a body as he has determined. . . ."

1 Corinthians 15:35–38

Paul is reticent about going into detail about the exact nature of the resurrection body of the believer, probably because of the paucity of revealed facts. Yet he does make several very definite statements. About such subjects the philosopher and the scientist can make only educated guesses. With the inspired Word in our hands, however, we have certainty.

1. It will be a *spiritual* body (1 Cor. 15:44), but will be perfectly adapted to our heavenly environment.

2. It will be a *real* body, not a phantom, but will be like that of the risen Christ, who challenged His disciples, "Touch me and see."

3. It will be a *recognizable* body, having identity with the physical body that has been laid to rest. After the resurrection Jesus spoke of having "flesh and bones." The Apostles recognized Jesus.

To clarify the issue, Paul then proceeds in 1 Corinthians 15 to draw comparisons and contrasts between the physical and the spiritual bodies.

4. It will be an *incorruptible* body (v. 42). It will be deathless, not subject to decay.

5. It will be a *glorious* body (v. 43), no longer "the body of our humiliation," subject to the tyranny of sin and the attacks of Satan.

6. It will be a *powerful* body (v. 43), having thrown off the frailty of its mortality.

While now the body is only an imperfect vehicle of the spirit and often frustrates it, in heaven the new body will be perfectly suited to conditions in its new sphere. "And just as we have borne the likeness of the earthly man, so shall we bear the likeness of the man from heaven" (1 Cor. 15:49).

It should be noted that the term *spiritual body* does not imply that it is ethereal and ghostly, but rather that it will be subject to the human spirit, not to our fleshly desires. In addition, the spiritual body will be able to express better the believer's aspirations than can the earthly body.

There are two current misconceptions about the spiritual body that need correction. (a) That it will be identical with the body that was buried. (b) That there is no organic connection between the body that was buried and that which is raised. If these conceptions were so, *there would need to be a new creation, not a resurrection*. We must acknowledge that there is mystery here, mystery that will be solved only in heaven.

In answering the question, "With what kind of body will they come?" Paul enunciated four truths, which are illustrated in the growth of a seed and in the diversity of animals and of the sun, moon, and stars.

1. What grows from the seed we sow is *not altogether identical* with what is sown (1 Cor. 15:37). An acorn produces not an acorn but an oak, yet both enjoy the same life force.

2. Each kind of seed has a *distinctive*, God-given body (Gen. 1:11; 1 Cor. 15:38).

3. The fruit of the seed sown has an *organic connection* with the seed from which it sprang. It is not a new creation but is the product of something already in existence.

4. There is great *diversity* in the bodies in the animal kingdom, as in the heavenly kingdom (1 Cor. 15:39–41).

If the resurrection body is not organically related to the body that is sown as it dies, there can be no resurrection. That we are unable to explain this does not alter its truth. We should keep in mind that there are other mysteries, perhaps connected, that we have to live with. Medical people tell us that in a lifetime our total body substance has been changed about ten times, and yet our personal identities have continued; we remain the same people. Our memory of past events remains unimpaired. This is a mystery, too, but it does shed some light on our problem.

In 1 Corinthians 15:42–44 Paul contrasts the old body with the new in four respects:

1. *It is sown perishable but will be raised imperishable* (v. 42).

There has been only one body not subject to corruption (Ps. 16:10; Acts 2:27). Sooner or later our physical bodies waste away. We all are victims of disease and, ultimately, death. Although the hearse is now ubiquitous, our spiritual bodies will be imperishable.

2. *It is sown in dishonor but will be raised in glory* (v. 43).

There is nothing beautiful or glorious about a decaying corpse. We dispose of it with respect in a grave or by cremation. But the resurrection body will be a glorious body, inconceivably more beautiful and wonderful. This is assured because "the Lord Jesus Christ, who, by the power that enables him to bring everything under his control, *will transform our lowly bodies so that they will be like his glorious body*" (Phil 3:20–21).

3. *It is sown in weakness but will be raised in power* (v. 43).

Inevitably the "strength of youth yields to the frailty of age. A dead body is a symbol of weakness, but our new body, like our Lord's will be characterized by power. Sleep will not be necessary to relieve weariness or recoup spent energy. Our abilities will be enlarged and we will throw off the limitations of which we are so conscious in life on earth." [33]

4. *It is sown a natural body; it will be raised a spiritual body* (v. 44).

The *natural body* is adapted to life in this world but is not fitted for life in the next. "The *spiritual body* is the organ which is intimately related to the spirit of man, just as his present body is intimately related to his earthly life." No longer will our bodies be subject to the laws that limit our physical life.

Our Lord's resurrection body is the pattern for ours (Phil. 3:21–22). He ate with His disciples (John 21:9, 12–13). He passed through closed doors (John 20:19). He appeared and disappeared from sight. He claimed to have flesh and bones (Luke 24:39). In other words, there was a real connection and identity with His former body, minus some of the limitations of that body.

The rendering, "our *vile* body" (Phil. 3:21) is one of the unhappier translations of the King James Version. "Our *lowly* body" is a more accurate interpretation. Our bodies are now subject to limitation and deterioration, they confine and cramp us, and they are destined to return to their constituent elements. But "we shall be changed." When our Lord returns, a glorious transformation will be effected. Our lowly bodies will become like His *glorious* body, and will be bodies in which our longings and aspirations will find perfect expression.

What was our Lord's resurrection body like?

It was certainly different from that same body before death.

1. There were three occasions when He was not recognized at first by His closest friends: "early in the morning, Jesus stood on the shore, but the disciples *did not realize* that it was Jesus" (John 21:4). "At this, she turned around and saw Jesus standing there, but she *did not realize* that it was Jesus" (John 20:14). "Jesus himself came up and walked along

with them; but they were *kept from recognizing him"* (Luke 24:15–16).

2. While the Lord's resurrection body was indeed different, it bore similarities to His physical body. He said He had "flesh and bones" (Luke 24:39). He denied that He was a ghost (Luke 24:37, 39). He prepared breakfast for His men and ate with them (John 21:9–14; Luke 24:42–43).

3. However, He was able to pass through closed doors (John 20:19). He was no longer confined by our limitations of time and space.

4. His was a *real* body. In answer to Thomas's disbelief, He extended the invitation, "Put your finger here; see my hands" (John 20:27). And to Mary, "Do not hold on to me" (John 20:17).

Jesus gave satisfying evidence that He was just the same person as before the Cross. He was recognized by His intimates who were now prepared to die for Him—as most of them did.

It is intriguing to note that our Lord's body retained its scars in the new body. Exactly what this signifies is difficult to say. One interesting suggestion is that scars received as suffering for Christ's sake will persist in some way, not as blemishes but as eternal badges of honor.

Will there be time in heaven?

"Then the angel I had seen standing on the sea and on the land raised his right hand to heaven. And he swore by him who lives forever and ever, who created the heavens and all that is in them, the earth and all that is in it, and the sea and all that is in it, and said, *'There will be no more delay!'* "

Revelation 10:5–6

In the King James Version of the Bible, the angel's announcement is translated, *"that there should be time no longer."* On the face of it, that would seem to indicate that there will be no time in heaven. This particular translation inspired the popular hymn of long ago:

> When the trumpet of the Lord shall sound
> *And time shall be no more*
> And the morning breaks eternal bright and fair
> When the saved of earth shall gather
> Over on the other shore,
> When the roll is called up yonder,
> I'll be there.

J. M. Black

But in reality that is not what the verse is saying. The translation of the Greek word for time, *chronos,* in verse 6 is unfortunate. Dr. A. T. Robertson, a noted Greek scholar, gives what is now the generally accepted meaning of the angel's proclamation:

> This does not mean that *chronos* (time), Einstein's "fourth dimension" (added to length, breadth, and height), will cease to exist, but only that there will be no more delay in the fulfillment of the seventh trumpet (verse 7) in answer to the question, "How long?" (6:10).[34]

The angel is merely saying that nothing can now hinder the fulfillment of the prophecy of verse 7. Most modern versions translate *chronos* as "delay" and not "time," and that interpretation fits the context. R. H. Mounce confirms this when he writes, "This is not the meaning of 'time' here. It would hardly be necessary for the angel to put himself under oath just to make the assertion about the timeless nature of eternity." [35] In the Buddhist *nirvana,* their version of heaven, time is done away with, but it is not as definite as that in the Christian heaven.

There are a number of roadblocks barring the way to the conclusion that in the age to come there will no longer be time or duration. Primary among them is that there is no clear statement to that effect in Scripture. Further, it would be difficult to imagine, for example, how there could be singing in heaven, or harp-playing, were there no such thing as time. Music without a beat? A new song without time? Maybe our problem is that we have only a "time" vocabulary to use.

Again, John speaks in Revelation 22:2 of the tree of life producing fruit every month. That would certainly breach the horticultural time cycle, but it clearly does not do away with time. The Scripture also speaks of "ages upon ages"—a succession of epochs of time.

May it be that only the *limitations* of time are absent from heaven? "Time is a necessary accompaniment of finitude," wrote G. H. Lang, "for no finite being can conceive infinity; hence time can never cease for the creature, though never needed by the Creator."

So it would appear that eternity will not annul time, but no finite mind can think in infinite terms. In heaven our minds will doubtless be geared to a different time frame than we now know in the physical universe. J. H. Bavinck makes a helpful suggestion: "The measurement of space and the computation of time will be entirely different on the other side of the grave than they are here, where miles and hours are our standard of measurement. But even the souls that dwell there will not become omnipresent like God."[36]

So we may tentatively conclude that there will be time in heaven, in the sense of movement from the present into the future, but it will not be time as we now know it.

FIVE

Heavenly Occupations

What will we do in heaven?
What place will music have?
What of the unevangelized?
Is salvation universal?

> In heaven we will not spend our time sitting on the
> edge of a cloud and playing a harp, or strolling the
> golden streets, or in picking flowers in a massive celes-
> tial garden. We will be busier than we have ever been,
> yet will do perfect work and never grow tired. We will
> each fulfill the inheritance God has given us and yet
> rest at the same time. God has built into human nature
> a drive to accomplish a goal and objective. One of life's
> greatest pleasures is satisfaction over a job well done. [37]
>
> *John Mac Arthur, Jr.*

Christian nations are the only ones which have real
music and often the most remarkable and the most joyous composers have been vital Christians: Bach and
Handel, to mention only two. Is not the heart delivered
from all fear and filled with the joy of the Holy Spirit
that can best express itself in song? Thus we are not
surprised to see the place that music occupies in the
description of heaven. . . . Throughout all eternity our
praise and anthems will mount up to Him who has
saved us. And the perfect harmony of heaven will go

far beyond the already sublime harmony of our earthly
music. [38]

Rene Pache

What will we do in heaven?

"The throne of God and of the Lamb will be in the
city, and his servants will serve him. They will see his
face. . . ."

Revelation 22:3–4

Most of what we are told about heaven, as we
have seen before, is couched in negative terms. Most
of its distinctive features lie in what is *not* there, but
we are not left without a description of positive features that make it eminently desirable. Some of these
are in the form of definite statements, like the verse at
the head of this chapter. Others are in alluring meta-
phors and symbols. Paul's assurance that heaven is
"better by far" than life here on earth guarantees us
full satisfaction in the life beyond.

Here are some of the ways in which we will be
occupied in heaven.

1. *"They will see his face, and his name will be on their
foreheads"* (Rev. 22:4).

This will be the zenith of heaven's joy and fulfillment. Christ will be the universal center of attraction.
Up to this time, people have been worshiping a God
who is only partially visible.

> Immortal, invisible, God only wise,
> In light inaccessible, hid from our eyes. . . .

But then we will have the unutterable joy of seeing
Him face-to-face with nothing between us.

In ancient Persia it was recorded that there were only seven men who "saw the king's face"—that is, had unrestricted access into his immediate presence. In our spiritual bodies we will be able to do what was denied to Moses in his earthly body. When Moses asked the Lord, "Now show me your glory," the answer he received was, "When my glory passes by, I will put you in a cleft in the rock and cover you with my hand until I have passed by. Then I will remove my hand and you will see my back; *but my face must not be seen*" (Ex. 33:18, 22–23). In heaven, however, beholding the glory of God in the face of Jesus Christ will be an everyday experience. We will walk every day "in the light of [His] presence" (Ps. 89:15).

At this glorious yet awesome prospect, we would identify with Thomas Binney when he wrote:

> O how shall I, whose native sphere
>   Is dark, whose mind is dim,
> Before the Ineffable appear,
> And on my naked spirit bear
>   That uncreated beam?

But with him, too, we can rejoice that:

> There is a way for man to rise
>   To that sublime abode,
> An offering and a sacrifice,
> A Holy Spirit's energies,
>   An advocate with God.

Apparently, the unfallen angels are able to bear the "uncreated beam," for Jesus said, ". . . their angels in heaven always see the face of my Father in heaven" (Matt. 18:10). Later, we will share with them that privilege.

The significance of the phrase in Revelation 22:4, "his name will be on their foreheads," is something we ought, also, to consider. The reference here is to the regalia of the high priest: "They made the plate, the sacred diadem, out of pure gold and engraved on it, like an inscription on a seal: Holy to the Lord. Then they fastened a blue cord to it to attach it to the turban, as the Lord commanded Moses" (Ex. 39:30–31).

In Jewish parlance a person's name stands for his or her character. So the plate on the turban of the high priest marked him out as a holy man, totally dedicated to God, and one who was to be like Him in character. We need not wait until we get to heaven to have this distinguishing mark.

2. "... *his servants will serve him*" (Rev. 22:3).

What an honor to serve the King of Kings and Ruler of the universe! But ours will be service of a special kind. One writer points out that "the words of this text are remarkable in that the Greek words for *servant* and *serve* are not related to one another as they are in the English language. The word *servant* means literally 'a slave,' but the word *serve* is reserved in Scripture for only one kind of service—the service of worship." [39] That is why some modern versions read, "His servants shall *worship* him." The Lamb of God on the throne will be the object of the adoring worship of the redeemed, who will render him, without reluctance, holy service.

3. "*And they will reign for ever and ever*" (Rev. 22:5).

This means that, in addition to the privilege of rendering priestly service, we will have royal status—sharing with Christ His glory. Was it not that for which He prayed? "Father, I want those you have given me to be with me where I am, and to see my glory" (John 17:24).

There are three classes of people who in Scripture are said to share the glory of the enthroned Christ.

(a) The first group includes *those who had remained loyal to Christ* amid the trials of this earthly life. Their service had not been perfect, but they had remained true despite opposition. "You are those who have stood by me in my trials. And I confer on you a kingdom, just as my Father conferred one on me, so that you may eat and drink at my table in my kingdom and sit on thrones, judging the twelve tribes of Israel" (Luke 22:28–30).

It should be noted that in the Greek there is no article in the clause "I confer on you a kingdom." It is literally, "I appoint to you kingdom," indicating royal rank and authority. As a recognition of their loyalty, they are accorded seats of honor at the heavenly banquet, sitting at His table. If we display a similar loyalty, we shall doubtless receive the same reward.

They will also "sit on thrones, judging the twelve tribes of Israel." In those days, as today, the king as supreme judge of the high court had legal assessors who sat with him, and no doubt this was the figure the Lord had in mind.[40]

(b) The second class of believers who reign with the Lord certainly includes *the martyrs for Christ*, and may possibly include all believers. "Do you not know that the saints will judge the world? And if you are to judge the world, are you not competent to judge trivial cases?" (1 Cor. 6:2). "I saw thrones on which were seated those who had been given authority to judge. And I saw the souls of those who had been beheaded because of their testimony for Jesus and because of the word of God" (Rev. 20:4).

(c) The third group includes *those who are the overcomers among the churches*. "To him who overcomes, I will give the right to sit with me on my throne, just as I overcame and sat down with my Father on his throne" (Rev. 3:21). "To him who overcomes and does my will to the end, I will give authority over the nations . . ." (Rev. 2:26).

Overcoming involves strife and struggle, and this promise is to those who have been faithful and have persevered in fighting the battles of the Lord. Paul had this in mind when he spoke of the crown laid up for him because he could say with truth, "I have fought the good fight, I have finished the race, I have kept the faith" (2 Tim. 4:7-8).

"In Revelation," writes John Gilmore, "Christians are active participators in world history. Reigning in heaven not only produces vindication of God's cause, it also means the prayers of the saints are coordinated with the execution of God's decrees." [41]

We should bear in mind, however that while we reign with Christ in glory, we will still remain His servants. In preparation for that day, we should emulate R. C. Halverson who likes to describe himself as "a servant of the Servant of the servants." Or, better still to follow the example of Him who, while still on earth, said, "I am among you as one who serves" (Luke 22:27).

4. *Heaven will be a worshiping community.*

The highest activity in heaven will be to ascribe to the triune God our spontaneous and unrestricted worship and adoration. The following paragraph is representative, in capsule form, of the worship that will be offered.

> Whenever the living creatures give glory, honor and thanks to him who sits on the throne and who lives for ever and ever, the twenty-four elders fall down before him who sits on the throne, and worship him who lives for ever and ever. They lay their crowns before the throne and say: "You are worthy, our Lord and God, to receive glory and honor and power, for you created all things, and by your will they were created and have their being."
>
> *Revelation 4:9–11*

It is an encouraging feature of the contemporary religious scene that increasing attention is being given to the importance of true worship in the life of the church, since this is to have priority in heaven.

Recently a fine young man of my acquaintance, the son of the principal of the Christian Leaders Training College in Papua, New Guinea, was drowned in a tragic accident. He was only seventeen years old, but Bradley Daimoi was spiritually mature beyond his years. Of the incident, the stricken but triumphant father wrote:

> While he was with us, he also belonged to the Lord. Now he is still with us, even though he is in the Lord's presence. Bradley has moved from one room to another. One day the barrier will be removed and we will see each other in the presence of the Lord for ever and ever.
>
> We were greatly comforted by the words of a song Bradley wrote before his home-going. It touched our hearts, and I trust it will touch your hearts also.

> I stood and wept in awful shock
>> for no one was good enough
> to open the scroll of the book of life,
>> no, no one could they find.
> They searched the heavens from end to end.
> They searched the sky and the sea and the land
> Not even under the earth was one to be found.
> Who is worthy? Is there anybody worthy?
> Then in a thousand tongues all the angels
>> sang aloud together:
> Worthy, worthy is the Lamb
>> to receive power and strength
>> and wisdom and wealth forever,
> For He is worthy, worthy to break the seals
> And He will open the holy scroll, praise His name!
>
> My heart was glad, my soul rejoiced
>> for someone was good enough.
> The slain Lamb, who died for all,
> The righteous one, the Holy God.
> I joined the angels and heavenly beings,
> I sang with every living thing
> For oh my hope was renewed, my future sure.
> Hallelujah, glory to the Lamb of God.
> Now and forevermore, I will always sing my
>> praises to Him.

What place will music have?

"They held harps given them by God and sang the song of Moses the servant of God and the song of the Lamb. . . ."

Revelation 15:2–3

When visiting the city of Lanchow in northwest China, I was puzzled and intrigued because the heavens were full of sweet music. I wondered if there were some aeolian harps somewhere, but the explanation was simple.

Many of the Chinese men owned flocks of racing pigeons. They used to make small pipes out of bamboo, each tuned to a different pitch. These they tied under the wings of their pigeons, and as the pigeons flew through the air, unconsciously they were making heavenly music. When I heard it, I recalled a hymn we used to sing in Sunday school:

> There is singing up in heaven
> Such as we have never known,
> Where the angels sing the praises
> Of the Lamb upon the throne;
> Their sweet harps are always tuneful
> And their voices always clear.
> O, that we might be more like them
> While we serve the Master here.
>> Holy, holy is what the angels sing,
>> And I expect to help them make
>> The courts of heaven ring;
>> But when I sing redemption's story,
>> They will fold their wings,
>> For angels never felt the joy
>> That our salvation brings.

Johnson Oatman

Music will indeed have a prominent place in the communal life of heaven, even as it did in Israel's tabernacle and temple. There were no fewer than 288 musicians engaged in the services of Solomon's temple (1 Chron. 25:1, 7). Vocal, choral, and instrumental music add to the worship of the congregation. Among the instruments mentioned in connection with the temple service are cymbals, psalteries, harps, trumpets, cornets, pipes, and other unspecified stringed instruments. An orchestra is no modern addition to the worship of the sanctuary! The twenty-four elders are depicted as each one having a harp, apparently accompanying themselves as they sing the praises of God (Rev. 5:8–9).

Christina Rosetti once remarked that heaven is revealed to earth as the homeland of music. What glorious music will enhance the felicity of heaven! There no one will be tone deaf or lack musical appreciation! If choirs and orchestras can elevate us to such heights of aesthetic enjoyment here on earth, what will it be like when we hear the celestial choirs accompanied by heaven-trained orchestras?

The apostle John had a foretaste of heaven's majestic music and struggled to convey the impression it made on him: "And I heard a sound from heaven like the roar of rushing waters and like a loud peal of thunder. The sound I heard was like that of harpists playing their harps. And they sang a new song before the throne" (Rev. 14:2–3).

It was a new song, because heaven's songs never grow hackneyed. We soon tire of oft-repeated choruses. We tend to go into neutral when singing hymns we have sung from our youth. But heaven's music and song is always fresh and new. No discordant note will ever jar on the ear there.

Music has been called the universal language, for it occurs in every culture. I remember well that once when traveling in China we left the main road and for three days rode on horseback over rough mountain tracks, until we came to a village called Kopu in the Kweichow province. It was only a small group of mudbrick houses in a tribal area. A weekend conference was going on, attended by about a thousand tribal people from adjoining areas. They were a very musical group, and to my amazement these primitive people in the heart of China presented "The Hallelujah Chorus" (in Chinese) from Handel's *Messiah.* They had boy sopranos, and the production was very creditable. I was quite moved as group after group presented their contributions in praise of the Savior. I had never expected to hear such music from unsophisticated tribal people.

From the glimpses of heaven given in the book of Revelation, it would appear that, if one were not singing, one would feel rather out of it, for singing is clearly the "in" exercise. Throughout the book of Revelation, as in the conference in China, different groups at appropriate moments bring their own musical contribution in praise to God.

The fact that they were singing "a new song" might indicate that heaven's music will be different from earth's, although God is the creator of both. We all have our preferences and aversions in music, but we can be sure that the music of heaven will be so melodious, so harmonious, so aesthetically pleasing and uplifting that no one's taste will be offended. We can anticipate some pleasant surprises in the musical realm. But we should bear in mind that

> Not all the harps above
> Could make a heavenly place,
> Should Christ His residence remove,
> Or but conceal His face.

There is one notable omission from the record; no mention is made of a conductor of the choir. The singing seems to be spontaneous. Doxologies seem to flow naturally. "Music leads us to the verge of the infinite, and lets us gaze on that," said Thomas Carlyle.

In referring to one of the songs Mark Twain considered so boring, Revelation 5:7–14, William Barclay termed it, "The greatest choir of praise the universe can ever hear," with wave after wave of joyous praise to God, until all created beings lift up their voices in one climactic song of praise: "To him who sits on the throne and to the Lamb be praise and honor and glory and power, for ever and ever."

> There was music in the heavens
> At the dawning of the days,
> When the morning stars together
> Sang their great Redeemer's praise,
> But the music that surpasses
> All this earth has heard and known,
> Will ring out when all the ransomed
> Gather round the Savior's throne.

W. M. Czamanski

What of the unevangelized?

"For since the creation of the world God's invisible qualities—his eternal power and divine nature—have been clearly seen, being understood from what has been made, *so that men are without excuse.*"

Romans 1:20

". . . when Gentiles, who do not have the law, do by nature things required by the law, they are a law for themselves, even though they do not have the law, *since they show that the requirements of the law are written on their hearts,* their consciences also bearing witness, and their thoughts now accusing, now even defending them."

Romans 2:14–15

One cannot study the subject of heaven without

pondering its relation to the unevangelized peoples who have not heard the gospel. Will they go to heaven?

It can be stated with confidence that no pagan will miss heaven simply because he or she has never heard the gospel. There is no scriptural support for that view. If pagans are "lost" in the biblical sense of the term as Jesus used it, it is not for that reason. It will be for the same reason that you and I were lost. Paul made this crystal clear. They—and we—are lost *because we are sinners,* born with a sinful nature. Further, we and they, sophisticate and pagan alike, have committed voluntary acts of sin. There is no difference between one class of people and another in this regard. Pagans have consciences and the light of conscience against which they have sinned. "This righteousness from God comes through faith in Jesus Christ to all who believe. *There is no difference, for all have sinned and fall short of the glory of God*" (Rom. 3:22–23).

"Men are in this plight," wrote R. E. Speer, "not because they are unevangelized, but because they are men. Sin is the destroyer of the soul, and the destruction of the knowledge of God which is life. And it is not the failure to have heard the gospel which makes them sinners."

Jesus seems to close the door to hope that anyone could see or enter the kingdom of heaven except through experiencing the new birth. Hear His words to Nicodemus: "I tell you the truth, *no one* can see the kingdom of God unless he is born again. . . . You should not be surprised at my saying, 'You must be born again' " (John 3:3, 7). In this passage being born again is presented as a prerequisite for entering heaven. John elsewhere states that the condition for entering heaven is that one's name is written in the Book of Life. Are these two experiences something that happen to pagans automatically and without their knowledge? (see Rev. 20:15).

In writing to the Ephesian Christians, Paul reminded them of their condition in their pagan days in these terms: ". . . remember that at that time you were separate from Christ, excluded from citizenship in Israel. . . *without hope and without God in the world*" (Eph. 2:12).

After exhaustive study of the relevant Scriptures, I have been unable to discover *any unequivocal body of Scripture* to support the view that anyone, including pagans, can enter heaven in any way other than through the door of new birth. Nor can I find scriptural support for the claims of universalism, which we will consider in the next chapter.

Of course the degree of responsibility of the pagan is immeasurably less than that of those who have had the benefit of gospel light. Since God is a righteous and impartial judge, we can be sure that His judgment will take into full account the degree of people's moral responsibility, which is known alone to Him. In the light of Calvary, we can have confidence that our compassionate God will make generous allowance for every extenuating circumstance, and any punishment will be only in accordance with the gravity of the sin. His mercy will be extended to pagans, as to all humanity, insofar as it can in justice be granted.

In his book *The Inspiration and Authority of Scripture*, Dr. Rene Pache, an evangelical theologian from Switzerland, has this to say on our subject:

Can a heathen who has received only the revelations

of nature and of conscience come to salvation? Paul expressly declares that everyone will be judged according to the light he has received. "All who sin apart from the law will also perish apart from the law, and all who sin under the law will be judged by the law" (Romans 2:12).

We have seen that the revelations of nature and conscience are sufficient to produce on the part of the heathen repentance and worship and the full responsibility for both. However, God who is omniscient knows perfectly whether a sincere yet ignorant man, given a chance to accept salvation, would take it or not. Christ died for the sins of the whole world, those committed before His coming as well as in times and places not reached with the gospel (cf. Romans 3:25). The Lord, then, will know how to treat every sinner according to His love and righteousness.[42]

But even if this is so it does not exempt us from the responsibility our Lord laid on us to "go and make disciples of all nations" (Matt. 28:19).

What is our responsibility?

If what is written in this section is the true scriptural teaching concerning the spiritual condition of the unevangelized heathen, then how *urgent* is our responsibility to make the Good News known to all men and women as speedily as possible. To have the knowledge of Christ and His salvation imposes on us an inescapable obligation to share that knowledge with everyone, as far as lies in our power, and that without delay. The harvest does not await the convenience of the farmer.

It has been said cogently that even if we were *academically uncertain* about the probable fate of those who have never heard about Christ, the parable of the lost sheep gives us reason to act. It lays down the principle that if we are convinced of the fate of as little as one percent of humanity, we are under obligation to seek the lost, even at utmost peril and cost to ourselves, that they might share with us the bliss of heaven. Our responsibility for the salvation of the heathen will be as great as our ability and opportunity to give them the gospel, or to make it possible for the gospel to be brought to them.

I was much moved many years ago when I met a little old woman in the Philippines. She was the first convert in her tribe, and she had opened her heart to Christ almost as soon as she had heard the gospel. When she was being baptized, the man who was conducting the service asked her, "Do you believe that Jesus Christ died on the cross to atone for your sins?" She gave an affirmative answer. "And do you believe that He rose again from the dead?"

"Of course I do," she replied, "And *wouldn't I have believed sooner if you had come sooner?*"

How many such potential disciples of Christ are waiting for someone to bring them the Good News of a Savior's love? Has the reader seriously faced his or her personal responsibility in this regard?

Is salvation universal?
"Salvation is found in *no one else,* for there is *no other name* under heaven given to men by which we must be saved."

Acts 4:12

Another question that confronts us is this: *Is there a second opportunity for salvation after death, for those who have not availed themselves of that priceless boon in this life?*

The view that has come to be known as *universalism* would contend that there is. This system of thought maintains that ultimately, since God is love, His love must triumph over His wrath. Proponents contend that, if there is such a thing as the wrath of God, it must prevail only temporarily. Since God is love, every human being will ultimately find himself or herself within the embrace of that love. Heaven surely would not be perfect were any excluded.

In his book *The Bible Today,* noted Bible scholar Dr. C. H. Dodd expressed the universalistic position succinctly: "As every human being lies under God's judgment, so every human being is destined, in his mercy, to eternal life."

That Christ is *potentially* the Savior of all by virtue of the fact that He made propitiation for the sins of the whole world when He died on the cross, no one could deny, especially in the face of 1 John 2:1–2: ". . . we have one who speaks to the Father in our defense— Jesus Christ, the Righteous One. He is the atoning sacrifice for our sins, and not only for ours but also for the sins of the whole world."

But it is maintained consistently throughout Scripture that the salvation He thus made *possible*, becomes *actual* and *effectual* only in response to a living faith. "For it is by grace you have been saved, *through faith*—and this not from yourselves, it is the gift of God—not by works, so that no one can boast" (Eph. 2:8–9).

There are large tracts of Scripture, preeminently in the teaching of our Lord, that run entirely counter to universalism. Throughout the Bible there is a consistent contrast drawn between good and evil, eternal life and eternal death, light and darkness, the sheep and the goats, the righteous and the wicked, the condemned and the uncondemned, heaven and hell. The contrasts are in black and white, without the slightest hint of the neutral gray of universalism, which summarily wipes out all distinctions.

It is taught in Scripture that there is complete and final separation of the saved from the lost:

> Enter through the narrow gate. For wide is the gate and broad is the road that leads to destruction, and many enter through it. But small is the gate and narrow the road that leads to life, and only a few find it.
>
> *Matthew 7:13–14*

> Then they will go away to *eternal punishment,* but the righteous to *eternal life.*
>
> *Matthew 25:46*

> If anyone's name was not found written in the book of life, he was thrown into the lake of fire.
>
> *Revelation 20:15*

There are five strong reasons why the teaching of universalism should be rejected as contrary to Scripture.

1. It repudiates the final authority of Scripture.
2. It virtually denies freedom to the human will.
3. It minimizes the gravity of sin.
4. It vitiates the biblical teaching on the final judgment.
5. It robs evangelistic preaching of its urgency and the missionary enterprise of a powerful motive.

In the light of the above biblical evidence, it is clear

that the hope of a second opportunity for salvation after death has no support in Scripture.

SIX

Second Advent and Judgment

What will the Second Advent and the judgment mean to us?
What will the Second Advent mean to Christ?
What will the Second Advent mean to Satan?

> The revelation of a Judgment Seat for believers is a further evidence that the fullness of heaven is not entered upon and enjoyed by any until after the advent and the resurrection. Christians who throughout these nineteen hundred years have passed on, have not yet been judged as to their faithfulness or unfaithfulness. That does not take place when we die, but will do so on the eve of the consummation of redemption, of that state which will be perfect, serviceable and eternal. [43]
>
> *W. Graham Scroggie*

What will the Second Advent and the judgment mean to us?

"Do not be amazed at this, for a time is coming when all who are in their graves will hear his [the Son of Man's] voice and come out—those who have done good will rise to live, and those who have done evil will rise to be condemned."

John 5:28–29

117

Parousia is the word used most frequently to denote the second advent of Christ. It occurs twenty-four times in the New Testament. Peter used it in connection with the Lord's first coming—undoubtedly a historical event. ". . . we told you about the power and coming (*Parousia*) of our Lord Jesus Christ" (2 Peter 1:16).

While the basic idea of the word is "presence," it means much more than that. As Louis Berkhof has said, "It points to the coming that precedes the presence." It refers to a bodily rather than a spiritual presence. The word was also applied to Paul. His detractors said of him, "His letters are weighty and forceful, but in person (*parousia*) he is unimpressive and his speaking amounts to nothing" (2 Cor. 10:10).

When in olden times a king or emperor planned to visit a city, elaborate preparations were made, as in our day, for the *parousia* of the important visitor. The early Christians were familiar with this use of the word and employed it in that sense to describe the arrival of Christ as King of Kings in power and glory.

"The *parousia* of Christ denotes His coming from heaven, which will be . . . a revelation of His glory, for the salvation of His church, for vengeance on His enemies, for the overthrow of opposition raised against Himself, and finally to realize the plan of salvation."

It is safe to conclude that, in every case where the term *parousia* is used, it refers to the coming of a person or a group. This assures us that when our Lord returns, He will come in "his glorious body" (Matt. 25:40; Phil. 3:21; 1 Thess. 4:15–17; 2 Thess. 2:1).

The promised second advent of our Lord will mean for us the beginning of the promised joys of heaven. It will mean being with Christ, which is better by far. But that will not be the whole story. It will precipitate the greatest series of judgmental events in the history of the world. Paul foretold a resurrection of the righteous and the wicked, when all will face the outcome of deeds done in the body (Acts 24:15).

The prospect of a coming Day of Judgment is one of the least popular articles of the Christian faith and is denied even by some who claim to be Christians. But it is not a concept that is peculiar to Christianity; it is common to other religions and philosophies as well. The Buddhist, for example, has his sixteen hells. The universal conscience of humanity bears witness to a sense of guilt, a feeling of moral responsibility to a supreme being or god. To God people are accountable, and He will reward good and punish evil.

The distinctive tenet of Christianity is that God has delegated this office to His Son, Jesus Christ, who will judge the living and the dead. "Moreover, the Father judges no one, but has entrusted all judgment to the Son" (John 5:22). "He [Jesus of Nazareth] commanded us to preach to the people and to testify that he is the one whom God appointed as judge of the living and the dead" (Acts 10:42).

No one who accepts the authority of Christ and the authenticity of His Word can doubt that there is a judgment to come. But there is a vast difference between the judgment of believers and that of nonbelievers. For the believer, there lies ahead the *bema* or judgment seat of Christ (2 Cor. 5:10). For the impenitent, there is the inescapable prospect of standing before the Great White Throne of judgment (Rev. 20:11).

It is neither possible nor necessary to compile an exact timetable for these awesome events; it is the absolute certainty of them that is important. ". . . man is destined to die once, and after that to face judgment" (Heb. 9:27). We must bear in mind that when these events do take place, the measures of time and space as we now know them will have no relevance.

But, speaking in terms with which we are familiar, would it not be reasonable to conclude that, since the "day of salvation" has extended over two millennia, we need not try to compress the Day of Judgment into a brief period? Conversely, does this judgment necessarily *require* a long time as we know it? In these days of the marvels of the computer world and television and the immeasurably greater marvel of the human brain, coupled with the omniscience of God, the slowness of our judicial processes affords no comparison. It is a well-established phenomenon that, in crisis, the whole content of a life may be flashed before the mind of a person in a moment of time.

In this book we are concerned only with the judgment of believers at the *bema*. This is one of the most important events connected with the return of Christ, so far as the believer is concerned. "For we must all appear before the judgment seat of Christ, that each one may receive what is due him for the things done while in the body, whether good or bad" (2 Cor. 5:10).

Does this mean that we will have to wait until that day to know whether we are saved or lost? Does Scripture not teach that upon believing in Christ we pass from death to life and will not come into condemnation?

Indeed it does. The explanation of 2 Corinthians 5:10 lies in the fact that Scripture recognizes two kinds of judgment. There is the judgment in criminal proceedings where the *judge* sits on the bench, hears the evidence, and decides the guilt, condemnation, or acquittal of the person charged. Then there is the judgment of the *umpire*, or *referee* who, as at the Olympic games, ascends his judgment seat to pronounce the winner and award the prize, because the victor has run fairly and well. Of course, the corollary is that those who have not run fairly and well "suffer loss" and win no prize. It is this second judgment seat that Paul has in view in this verse.

A person's eternal destiny is already determined in this life, according to whether or not he or she has trusted Christ for salvation. "So then, each of us will give an account of himself to God" (Rom. 14:12). Few verses of Scripture are more soul-searching than this. Daniel Webster, the noted American statesman, on being asked what was the greatest thought he had ever entertained, replied, "The greatest thought that has ever entered my mind is that one day I will have to stand before a holy God and give an account of my life."

The judgment seat of Christ, then, is His "umpire" seat. The primary purpose of His judgment is to assess and reward believers for the manner in which they have used their opportunities and discharged their responsibilities. The basis on which we will be judged is stated in clear terms: "that each one may receive what is due him *for the things done while in the body*, whether good or bad."

But *motives* as well as deeds will be taken into account. "Therefore judge nothing before the appointed time; wait till the Lord comes. He will bring to light what is hidden in darkness and *will expose the motives of men's hearts"* (1 Cor. 4:5).

In a very penetrating paragraph Paul tells us how this process is carried out:

> . . . no one can lay any foundation other than the one already laid, which is Jesus Christ. If any man builds on this foundation using gold, silver, costly stones, wood, hay or straw, his work will be shown for what it is, because the Day will bring it to light. It will be revealed with fire, and the fire will test the quality of each man's work. If what he has built survives, *he will receive his reward.* If it is burned up, *he will suffer loss;* he himself will be saved, but only as one escaping through the flames.
>
> *1 Corinthians 3:11–15*

Whatever else this paragraph teaches, it makes clear that there can be a saved soul but a lost life, because of unfaithfulness in the stewardship of life.

What do gold, silver, and costly stones symbolize? It is well to examine this subject in view of the serious possibilities implicit in the passage. What will be taken into account in the assessment?

1. Our testimony to Christ—Philippians 2:16.
2. Our suffering for Christ—1 Peter 4:13.
3. Our faithfulness to Christ—Luke 12:42–43; Revelation 2:10.
4. Our service for Christ—1 Corinthians 3:8; Hebrews 6:10.
5. Our generosity to Christ—2 Corinthians 9:6; 1 Timothy 6:17–19.

6. Our use of time for Christ—Ephesians 5:15–16; Colossians 4:5.
7. Our exercise of spiritual gifts—Matthew 25:14–28; 1 Peter 4:10.
8. Our self-discipline for Christ—1 Corinthians 9:24–25.
9. Our winning of souls for Christ—1 Thessalonians 2:19.

The awards conferred by our Lord from His umpire seat are referred to under the figure of crowns. (These are dealt with in our section on rewards, beginning on page 77.)

But the *bema* is not all joy and the winning of prizes for all believers. Paul told the Corinthian Christians that, just as the stars differ in glory, so also will the saints (1 Cor. 15:41–42).

Some will be ashamed when He comes because of unfaithfulness to Him, of persistence in known sin, or of having been ashamed of Him before people. "And now, dear children, continue in him, so that when he appears we may be *confident and unashamed* before him at his coming" (1 John 2:28).

Some will suffer loss because they have used wood, hay, and straw in building on the foundation, and these materials cannot withstand fire. As F. E. Marsh has said,

> They have built the material of earth's products upon the foundation of Christ's being and work. The gold of Christ's deity, the silver of his vicarious sacrifice, and the precious stones of his peerless worth and coming glory, are truths that will stand the tests of God's fire; but the wood of self-esteem, the hay of man's frailty,

and the straw of human eloquence will all be burnt up,
although the worker himself will be saved.

"If [any man's work] is burned up, he will suffer loss;
he himself will be saved, but only as one escaping
through the flames" (1 Cor. 3:15).

Will we be among those who receive the full reward and have an abundant entrance into Christ's
kingdom, or will we be among those who are
ashamed and suffer loss?

What will the Second Advent mean to Christ?

*"Father, I want those you have given me to be with me
where I am, and to see my glory,* the glory you have giv-
en me because you loved me before the creation of
the world."

John 17:24

The inherent selfishness of even the regenerate
human heart is disclosed by our tendency to think of
the Lord's return more in terms of what it will mean
to us—how the accompanying events will affect us—
than of what it will mean to Him. A very popular
hymn of a generation ago epitomized that sentiment:

> O that will be glory for me
> Glory for me, glory for me
> When by His grace I will look on His face,
> That will be glory, be glory for me.

We are rightly thrilled at the thought of our magnificent inheritance in Christ, but are we equally
thrilled at the thought of His inheritance in us? Here
is Paul's prayer: "I pray also that the eyes of your
heart may be enlightened in order that you may know

the hope to which he has called you, *the riches of his glorious inheritance in the saints,* and his incomparably great power for us who believe" (Eph. 1:18–19).

What thought we have given to *His glorious inheritance in us?* Do we pay sufficient attention to His eager expectation and anticipation of His wedding day? Is His coronation day prominent in our minds?

> He is waiting with long patience
> For His crowning day,
> For that Kingdom which shall never
> Pass away,
> Watching till His royal banner
> Floateth far and wide,
> Till He seeth of His travail,
> Satisfied!
>
> *A. J. Janvrin*

Consider the startling contrast between His first advent and His second. Then He came in poverty and humiliation; soon He will come with incredible riches and glory. Then He came in weakness; soon He will come in great power. Then He came in loneliness; soon He will come accompanied by His hosts of angels and the company of the redeemed. Then He came as a man of sorrows; soon He will come with radiant and unalloyed joy. Then in mockery men placed a reed in His hand; soon He will wield the scepter of universal dominion. Then men pressed a crown of acanthus thorns upon His brow; soon He will come adorned with the many diadems He has won. Then He was blasphemed, denied, betrayed; soon every knee will bow to Him, acknowledging Him as King of Kings and Lord of Lords.

In His prayer to His Father, He made only one personal request: "I want those you have given me to be with me where I am, and to see my glory" (John 17:24). This prayer reveals the deep yearning of His heart. These failing men meant a great deal to Him— and so do we. When He comes again, this yearning will have its fulfillment, "and so we will be for ever with the Lord." But in the light of His greatness and majesty and holiness, do we not cry out with the psalmist in amazed wonder, ". . . what is man that you are mindful of him, the son of man that you care for him?" (Ps. 8:4).

When He comes again, He will be fully satisfied with the outcome of His so costly sacrifice; "He shall see of the travail of his soul, and shall be satisfied" (Isa. 53:11 KJV). He will then experience the consummation of "the joy set before him."

The noted Rabbi Duncan of Edinburgh once preached on the text, "he shall see his seed" (Isa. 53:10 KJV). He divided the text as follows:

He shall see them born and brought in.
He shall see them educated and brought up.
He shall see them supported and brought
    through.
He shall see them glorified and brought home.

This is part of the joy set before Him.

Christ's return will result in His eternal union with His bride, the church, which He purchased with His own blood. For Him, as for us, that will mean the ecstatic joy of the wedding supper of the Lamb and eternal fellowship and communion.

When He returns, it will be to receive the kingdom of which He spoke so much on earth. When He first came to His own people and offered Himself as their king, their response was, "we will not have this man to reign over us." But at last His kingship will be universally acknowledged and confessed.

> O, the joy to see Thee reigning,
>   Thee, my own beloved Lord!
> Every tongue Thy name confessing,
> Worship, honor, glory, blessing,
>   Brought to Thee with one accord;
> Thee my Master and my Friend,
>   Vindicated and enthroned,
> Unto earth's remotest end
>   Glorified, adored and owned.
>
> *F. R. Havergal*

What will the Second Advent mean to Satan?

"Now have come the salvation and the power and the kingdom of our God, and the authority of his Christ. For the accuser of our brothers, who accuses them before our God day and night, has been hurled down."

Revelation 12:10

For no one will the return of Christ have greater and more far-reaching significance than for Satan, the evil prince of this world. Scripture presents a consistent picture of two rival kingdoms confronting each other on the world scene—the kingdoms of Satan and darkness and the kingdom of God and light. Satan and his minions are allied with evil people in their plan to smash the kingdom of God and effect the ruin of the human race.

At the end of the age, Satan is seen in alliance with the beast and the false prophet. These three, united in a common purpose to defeat Christ and secure domination of the whole world, form a sinister trinity of evil. While on earth, Jesus inflicted a stunning defeat on Satan—first in the temptation in the desert, but preeminently in the Cross. Christ "shared in [our] humanity so that by his death he might destroy him who holds the power of death—that is, the devil—and free those who all their lives were held in slavery by their fear of death" (Heb. 2:14–15).

It was for this very purpose that Christ came to earth the first time: "He who does what is sinful is of the devil, because the devil has been sinning from the beginning. *The reason the Son of God appeared was to destroy the devil's work*" (1 John 3:8).

At Calvary that victory was achieved gloriously, and the sentence of doom was passed. The blessed result was that, "having disarmed the powers and authorities, he made a public spectacle of them, triumphing over them by the cross" (Col. 2:15).

Ever since Calvary, the vaunted power of the adversary has been shattered. His power is not inherent, it is derived. He is not invincible but vulnerable. He is not triumphant but doomed. He and his accomplices are reserved for a final and future judgment, which is described in Revelation 20:7–10:

> When the thousand years are over, Satan will be released from his prison and will go out to deceive the nations in the four corners of the earth—Gog and Magog—to gather them for battle. . . . They marched across the breadth of the earth and surrounded the camp of God's people, the city he loves. But fire came

down from heaven and devoured them. And *the devil, who deceived them, was thrown into the lake of burning sulfur,* where the beast and the false prophet had been thrown. They will be tormented day and night for ever and ever.

So one of the blessed absences from heaven will be Satan the tempter, the accuser, the deceiver. There will be no more temptations directed at the weak spots of our nature. No more raking up of old sins and unfounded accusations. No more deceptions playing on our ignorance and credulity. Nothing unclean or defiling will ever enter heaven through those pearly gates. Hallelujah!

SEVEN

New Heavens and New Jerusalem

The new heavens and the new earth
The new Jerusalem
The wedding supper of the Lamb
How to gain entrance to heaven
Three testimonies

The first heavens and the first earth have passed away.
In our imagination let us try to see this new universe.
The very foundations of the earth have been subjected
to purifying fire. Every stain of sin, every trace of death
has been removed. Out of the great conflagration a new
universe has been born. The word used in the original
implies that it was a "new" but not an "other" world. It
is the same heaven and earth, but gloriously rejuvenated, with no weeds, thorns or thistles. Nature comes
into its own.

William Hendriksen[44]

God is the architect and contractor; no archangel's
matchless taste and incomparable genius were used in
drafting the plan of this glorious city. God drew the
plan. The stores of God's own wisdom and skill, and
faultless taste brought into perfection the design of
heaven. God was the builder. Only He could carry out
the original.

> The God who laid the deep foundations of the world
> and brought into being its mighty movements stoops
> to enter again into the work of creation and builds a
> home for His children. [45]
>
> *Edward M. Bounds*

The new heavens and the new earth

"But in keeping with his promise, we are looking forward to a new heaven and a new earth, the home of righteousness."

2 Peter 3:13

"Then I saw a new heaven and a new earth, for the first heaven and the first earth had passed away, and there was no longer any sea."

Revelation 21:1

In this final series of visions granted to John, we have come to the climax of the purposes of God and to scenes that surpass the highest expectation of the saints. We are transported from time to eternity. Chapters 21 and 22 of Revelation are the most spectacular and dramatic of the whole book and portray a breathtaking picture of what heaven will be like.

Chapter 20 concludes with the words, "he was thrown into the lake of fire" (v. 15). But in the following two chapters, in striking contrast, we are presented with the glories and splendor of the heaven in which the redeemed will spend eternity.

The Hebrews had long cherished the dream of new heavens and a new earth where sin, sorrow, and suffering would be no more. The prophet Isaiah articulated that desire: "Behold, I will create new heavens and a new earth. The former things will not be remembered, nor will they come to mind" (Isa. 65:17).

John saw the new heavens and the new earth. He saw them in a vision then, but knew that they would come into reality in a day yet future. He saw a superworld, the home of righteousness, which God had promised through the prophets (Acts 3:21).

In flaming metaphor Peter foreshadows the method by which this tremendous metamorphosis and renovation will take place.

> But the day of the Lord will come like a thief. The heavens will disappear with a roar; the elements will be destroyed by fire, and the earth and everything in it will be laid bare. . . . That day will bring about the destruction of the heavens by fire, and the elements will melt in the heat. But in keeping with his promise we are looking forward to a new heaven and a new earth, the home of righteousness.
>
> *2 Peter 3:10–13*

The old physical earth that has been the center of so much sin, revolt, and bloodshed has disappeared in this vision, as have the heavens (not the heaven where God's throne is). Those heavens have been the sphere where Satan has carried on his activities. Because he pollutes everything he touches, they must be cleansed by fire.

Because this earth has also been the theater in which the drama of redemption has been enacted, it will, phoenix-like, rise from its ashes by the power of God, to a new and unimaginable glory. The old Jerusalem had been stained with the blood of prophets and martyrs, and, most shamefully of all, with the blood of God's Son. But no more blood will flow, and the New Jerusalem will be the home of the righteous.

It is interesting that the only qualifying statement in this passage about the new heavens and earth is that "there was no longer any sea" (Rev. 21:1). The sea is a symbol of unrest and instability. Earlier on in John's vision, it was from the sea that the satanic beast arose. "And I saw a beast coming out of the sea. He had ten horns and seven heads, with ten crowns on his horns, and on each head a blasphemous name" (Rev. 13:1). "Then the angel said to me, 'The waters you saw, where the prostitute sits, are peoples, multitudes, nations and languages' " (Rev. 17:15). The surging sea represents the nations of the world in their perennial conflict with one another. But in the rejuvenated heavens and earth all will be peace and serenity.

The picture is of a universe transformed, perfected, purged of everything that is evil and that exalts itself against God. It is "new," not in the sense of being a new creation, but of being new in character—a worthy milieu for the residence of God and His redeemed people. It is new because of the presence of a new community of people, utterly loyal to God and to the Lamb.

We cannot tell what the new creation will be like, for no details are given. The fact that there will be no more sea could be an indication that the whole order of nature will be changed.

In one of his sermons, Dean Henry Alford said, "The general tenor of prophecy, and the analogy of the divine dealings point unmistakably to this earth, purified and renewed, as the eternal habitation of the blessed."

Along the same lines, Alexander Maclaren wrote, "It seems to me that some cosmical change having passed upon this material world in which we dwell, it in regenerated form will be the final abode of redeemed humanity. That, I think, is the natural interpretation of a great deal of scriptural teaching."

The new Jerusalem
"I saw the Holy City, the new Jerusalem, coming down out of heaven from God, prepared as a bride beautifully dressed for her husband."

Revelation 21:2

"This famous description, the equal of which cannot be found in any other literature of the ancient world," is the way one writer terms the vision of the New Jerusalem recorded in Revelation 21. The new heavens and new earth must have a new metropolis in keeping with their dignity and splendor. And God will send it down from heaven—the Holy City, the New Jerusalem.

Is this a description of a literal city of gold and pearl and precious stones, or should John's vision be interpreted symbolically? Different scholars hold divergent views for which they can advance plausible arguments. In this connection, Dr. Wilbur M. Smith in an article on the subject writes,

One must not be dogmatic here as to what may be interpreted symbolically and what must be interpreted literally. Different views are held by scholars of equal devotion to the authority of Scripture. One writer who insists on a strong symbolism here, states that "the reason for the employment of symbolism here may be that there is simply no other way of creating in our minds any just conception of reality. [46]

A strong case for the symbolic interpretation is made by G. H. Lang in his *Revelation of Jesus Christ*; I quote it at length because it seems to accord more with the whole tenor of the book of Revelation than the opposing view. Lang feels that a literal interpretation is unacceptable because of inherent difficulties.

> Is it really to be believed that there exist vast masses of solid gold, of which angels have measuring rods and of which streets are made? If it be asserted that there are pearls so large that a single one suffices for a gate proportionate to a wall 230 feet high, we are induced to reflect how large must have been the oysters in which they grew. This opinion cannot be carried through consistently without doing violence to the figurative language. . . . "The river of the water of life" is incontestably a figure, namely, the Spirit of God (John 7:37–38). But this feature being a symbol, so will be that of a "tree that grows by the river."

With regard to the city itself, Lang writes,

> After reading various attempts to portray a literal city of this form and dimension, I still fail utterly to form the vaguest conception of an actual city as a cube, on every side as high as it is long and broad; or even as a pyramid, each slope of which is of the same length as its base line, or of a tapering tower as high as the length of its base line, with a street encircling it from base to summit.

He concludes with this assertion, with which I am inclined to agree: "That a city can be so shaped, is to me at least, so unimaginable as to decide that this chapter is not a description of anything concrete." [47] John is concerned with spiritual states, not material realities.

But these symbols and figures do have glorious reality behind them. The descent of the city, although expressed in terms of a vision, has deep spiritual significance and is intended to convey to our earthbound minds the unimaginable glory that awaits us in heaven.

What does the city represent?

John will tell us himself:

> One of the seven angels who had the seven bowls full of the seven last plagues came and said to me, "Come, I will show you the bride, the wife of the Lamb." And he carried me away in the Spirit to a mountain great and high, and showed me the Holy City, Jerusalem, coming down out of heaven from God. It shone with the glory of God. . . .
>
> *Revelation 21:9–11*

It should be noted that the angel did not undertake to *explain* the symbolism, but simply *showed* him the bride. The city was the bride!

There is a parallel to this in chapter 5:5–6:

> Then one of the elders said to me, "Do not weep! See, *the Lion* of the tribe of Judah . . . has triumphed. He is able to open the scroll and its seven seals."
> Then I saw *a Lamb*, looking as if it had been slain, standing in the center of the throne. . . .

The bride—a city. The lion—a Lamb.

I would submit that it is reasonable to infer that the city is a symbol of the ideal church as God conceived it in the beginning, and as it will be in the end—"without stain or wrinkle or any other blemish" (Eph. 5:27). The church as it is on earth now is only a poor shadow of the transcendent splendor of the church as it will be in the future.

In Revelation 21:1–4, 22–23, John enumerates some features of life on earth that will no longer be present in the Holy City—no more sea, tears, death, mourning, pain, no temple, no need of the light of sun or moon. As these absences from heaven have already been discussed in chapter 3, no further comment is necessary here, except to say that if we completely reverse the sadness and miseries of earth, we can gain some idea of the joys and bliss of heaven.

The central and most important feature of the New Jerusalem is announced from the throne: "And I heard a loud voice from the throne saying, '*Now the dwelling of God is with men*, and he will live with them. They will be his people, and God himself will be with them and be their God' " (Rev. 21:3–4).

Israel had known something of God's presence in its midst in the symbols of the ark of the covenant and in the pillar of cloud and fire, but it had forfeited that privilege through its repeated failure and apostasy. Now the promise made to the Hebrews in their desert journey finds full and glorious fulfillment: "I will look on you with favor.... I will put my dwelling place among you, and I will not abhor you. I will walk among you and be your God, and you will be my people" (Lev. 26:9–12).

"We have in this section (Rev. 21:1–22) a description of that which is ideal," writes William Hendriksen. He continues,

> Whatever is the result of God's redeeming grace, in the present or the future, is included here. The redeeming grace and transforming power of God must not be viewed as pertaining only to the future. No, here and now in this present era, it is already working in the hearts of God's children. Consequently, what we find here is *a description of the redeemed universe of the future, as foreshadowed by the redeemed church of the present.* [48]

In summary, the city of God and the new heavens and new earth are the climax of the whole scheme of redemption. God is not content with merely undoing the ravages that sin and Satan have wrought in the beautiful world He created. He creates a new world, the home of righteousness that far surpasses the one ruined by Satan. He could have recreated the original Eden, but that would have held the possibility of a repetition of the Fall, with all its tragic consequences. His plan is better by far. He establishes a new world and a new world order on the basis of the redemptive work of the Lamb of God, thus ensuring that there will be no recurrence of the evils that have plagued humanity. With Satan finally and forever bound and with nothing that defiles able to enter our heavenly home, we will indeed prove that to be with Christ in heaven is *better by far.*

> My Father's house on high,
>   Home of my soul, how near,
> At times to faith's foreseeing eye
>   Thy golden gates appear.

Ah! then my spirit faints
To reach the land I love,
The bright inheritance of saints,
Jerusalem above.

James Montgomery

The wedding supper of the Lamb

"Let us rejoice and be glad and give him glory! For the wedding of the Lamb has come, and his bride has made herself ready. . . .

"Then the angel said to me, 'Write: "Blessed are those who are invited to the wedding supper of the Lamb!" ' "

Revelation 19:7,9

This is the event for which all heaven is waiting—the final union between Christ and His chosen bride, the church. It is the event that the redeemed of every age have anticipated and longed for, an event that will add immeasurably to the felicity of heaven, the era for which creation groans and the children of God pray.

The introductory scene to the wedding opens with a great heavenly choir singing a hallelujah chorus. The lyric attributes glory and deliverance and power to God, because of His righteous judgment on the wicked and persecuting harlot church (Rev. 19:2–4)—a song rejoicing in the triumph of truth over error.

"Then I heard what sounded like a great multitude, like the roar of rushing waters and like loud peals of thunder, shouting: 'Hallelujah! For our Lord God Almighty reigns. Let us rejoice and be glad and give him glory!' " (Rev. 19:6–7). To understand the symbolism of this sublime passage, one requires a background of knowledge of the marriage customs of the East. A Jewish betrothal was considered much more binding than an engagement is in our culture. The betrothed couple was to most intents and purposes looked upon as already married. Infidelity during this period could lead to divorce (see 2 Cor. 11:2).

During the time between betrothal and the marriage ceremony, the bridegroom paid the customary marriage dowry to the father of the bride (see Gen. 34:12). It was a time of preparation and adornment of the bride, who "made herself ready" for the great event. In company with his friends, the bridegroom then proceeded to his own home or that of his parents. The climax was the solemn yet joyous wedding feast.

The imagery of marriage occurs frequently in both Testaments. Several of the Lord's parables centered around a wedding (Matt. 22:2–14; Mark 2:19–20). Paul made use of this figure in 2 Corinthians 11:2 and Ephesians 5:25–33.

Jesus Himself is, of course, the heavenly Bridegroom. The bride of whom John the Baptist spoke (John 3:29) is the true church, which includes all who have exercised saving faith in Christ. The marriage symbolism expresses the indissoluble union existing between Christ and His redeemed people.

But what of the devout Hebrews who believed while living under the old covenant? Are they included as elements of the bride? Because they looked forward to the atoning sacrifice of the Messiah, they do share in the salvation achieved by Christ. Jesus said, "Your father Abraham rejoiced at the thought of seeing my day; he saw it and was glad" (John 8:56).

Paul said concerning Abraham, "Abraham believed God, and it was credited to him as righteousness" (Rom. 4:3).

Jesus also said that "Abraham, Isaac and Jacob and all the prophets . . . will take their places at the feast in the kingdom of God" (Luke 13:28–29). The fact that "on the gates were written the names of the twelve tribes of Israel" (Rev. 21:12) indicate that the saints of Old Testament times are not excluded from the festivities.

Betrothal takes place with a view to the wedding day, the joyous climax to growing intimacy and communion. Christ chose His bride from all eternity, and His incarnation made possible her betrothal to Him. He paid the dowry, the bride-price, not in shining silver or yellow gold but in crimson drops of precious blood at Calvary. Then began the interval after which He will return to claim His bride, and take her to the glorious home He has prepared for her. During the interval, the bride makes herself ready (Rev. 19:7–8).

With regard to her wedding apparel, it should be noted that "fine linen, bright and clean, *was given her* to wear" (19:8). The wedding garments were customarily provided by the host who gave the feast. Even so, our heavenly Bridegroom provides the wedding attire, and the bride wears it. As Robert Murray McCheyne put it,

> When I stand before the throne,
> Dressed in beauty not my own
> Then Lord shall I fully know,
> Not till then how much I owe.

Our Lord's two parables of the wedding feast emphasize two important truths concerning the necessity of preparation for the coming of the Bride-groom. The parable of the wedding garment underscores the need for personal holiness (Matt. 22:1–14), and the parable of the ten virgins illustrates the necessity of being filled with the Holy Spirit (Matt. 25:1–13). We must make sure that we have received the wedding garment and that our lamps are filled with oil.

The Eastern wedding feast could last for a week or more. The wedding feast of the Lamb continues throughout eternity in the home He has gone to prepare.

> The bride eyes not her garment
> But her dear Bridegroom's face,
> I will not gaze at glory,
> But on my King of grace.
> Not at the crown He giveth
> But on His pierced hand,
> The Lamb is all the glory
> Of Immanuel's Land.
>
> *A. R. Cousins*

How to gain entrance to heaven
"I tell you the truth, unless you change and become like little children, you will never enter the kingdom of heaven."

Matthew 18:3

In the previous pages I think I have, to those who accept the authority of the Scriptures, presented a *prima facie* case for there being life after death and for the existence of such a place as the heaven of the Bible. There is no doubt that our Lord and His apostles taught these truths, and they also taught with equal clarity that there is such a place as hell, where the impenitent receive the reward of their deeds.

The popular idea, according to recent polls, is that good people go to heaven, and a majority of those polled rated their own chances of going there to be good. There are few who don't want to go to heaven. Most base their expectation on their performance in this life, irrespective of their relationship to Christ. Is this a valid hope?

Here again we are driven to the Scriptures for an authoritative answer. All else is speculation, but in a matter of such far-reaching importance, we need more than that, we want certainty.

In a world where there is so much injustice and inequality, where the righteous suffer and the evil prosper, where the weak are exploited and the powerful flourish, it is easy to conclude as Israel did that, on the surface at least, "The way of the Lord is not just" (Ezek. 18:25). In our contemporary society the administration of the judicial system too often gives the breaks to the criminal rather than to the victim. The greater number of crimes go unpunished, while meritorious action is often unrewarded. It is the two nations who instigated World War II who have prospered most since then. This creates a puzzling moral problem.

The psalmist Asaph, faced with a similar problem, had no answer and almost lost his faith. Hear him:

> But as for me, my feet had almost slipped; I had nearly lost my foothold. For I envied the arrogant when I saw the prosperity of the wicked.

They have no struggles; their bodies are healthy and strong. They are free from the burdens common to man; they are not plagued by human ills.

Psalm 73:2–5

Because of human sin, life on earth is manifestly unjust. If God is as good and just as the Scriptures state and as we have maintained, how can He retain His character while permitting such a state of affairs to continue? If He remains inactive in this situation, it would appear that He is either uncaring or is powerless to redress the manifest injustices of this life.

But both Scripture and history are replete with affirmations that He is neither uncaring nor inactive. This life is not the end of all. Such inequalities will be redressed.

Where did Asaph discover the solution to his problem? He tells us, "Surely in vain have I kept my heart pure; in vain have I washed my hands in innocence. . . . When I tried to understand all this, it was oppressive to me *till I entered the sanctuary of God*; then I understood their final destiny" (vv. 13, 16–17). Like him, we should take our perplexing problems into the presence of God and try to see things from His perspective. It is the end view that is important.

Scripture abounds with intimations that a day is coming when injustices will be redressed and inequalities straightened out, when evil will be punished and virtue appropriately rewarded. This will take place at the Day of Judgment. Those who in this life have not availed themselves of the only way of salvation through the grace of God and the atoning death of Christ will not enter the gates of heaven. The Word is unequivocal: "Nothing impure will ever enter it, nor will anyone who does what is shameful or deceitful, but *only those whose names are written in the Lamb's book of life"* (Rev. 21:27).

The Lamb's Book of Life

What does it mean to have one's name written in the Lamb's Book of Life?

The metaphor of books of record occurs throughout Scripture, beginning with Moses' plea to God to be "blotted out" of God's book as an atonement for the sins of the people of Israel (Ex. 32:32). This figure of speech is drawn from the registers of the tribes of Israel. Its final appearance is in the text we are considering.

Concerning the judgment in front of the Great White Throne, we read, "Then I saw a great white throne. . . . And I saw the dead, great and small, standing before the throne, *and books were opened. Another book was opened, which is the book of life. The dead were judged according to what they had done as recorded in the books"* (Rev. 20:11–12).

One set of books, then, contains the record of each person's life-history. The other book is the Lamb's Book of Life. The first record can bring only condemnation, for all have fallen short of God's standards. In the Book of Life are recorded the names of those who have repented of their sins and exercised saving faith in Christ as Redeemer and Savior.

"Remember that it depends on ourselves whether our names are written there or not. John Bunyan in his *Pilgrim's Progress* describes the armed man who came up to the table where the man with the book and the inkhorn was seated, and said, 'Set down my name.' " It is open to anyone to do just that. A living faith in Christ, the Lamb of God who "takes away the sin of the world," is the sole condition for having our names written in that book, and that constitutes our passport through the pearly gates. "They that trust in Jesus Christ," writes Alexander Maclaren "shall have their names written in the Book of Life; graven on the High Priest's breastplate, and inscribed on His mighty hand and His faithful heart."

Why not make absolutely certain of heaven by opening your heart to Christ the Savior and Lord right now, inviting Him to enter, to cleanse it from sin, and to make it His permanent dwelling-place? Make the following poem the prayer of your heart, and He gives this assurance, "If anyone hears my voice and opens the door, I will come in and eat with him, and he with me" (Rev. 3:20).

> Come in O come! the door stands open now,
> I knew Thy voice, Lord Jesus it was Thou;
> The sun has set long since, the storms begin,
> 'Tis time for Thee, my Savior, O come in!
>
> Alas, ill-ordered shews the dreary room;
> The household stuff lies heaped amid the gloom,
> The table empty stands, the couch undressed;
> Ah! what a welcome for the Eternal Guest!
>
> I seek no more to alter things, or mend,
> Before the coming of so great a Friend;
> All were at best unseemly; and 'twere ill
> Beyond all else to keep Thee waiting still.
>
> Come, not to find, but make this troubled heart
> A dwelling worthy of Thee as Thou art;

To chase the gloom, the terror and the sin;
Come, all Thyself, yea come Lord Jesus in.

Handley C. G. Moule

Three testimonies

We conclude our study with testimonies of three who experienced the new birth, had their names written in the Lamb's Book of Life, and are now in heaven.

In the middle of this century, *Dr. Harry Rimmer* was known throughout the Christian world for his books on the Bible and science. A week or two before Dr. Rimmer died in 1953, Dr. Charles Fuller, sponsor of the Old Fashioned Revival Hour, was scheduled to speak about heaven on the next Sunday. During the week he received a letter from Dr. Rimmer, of which this is part:

Next Sunday you are to talk about Heaven. I am interested in that land, because I have held a clear title to a bit of property there for more than fifty-five years. I did not buy it. It was given to me "without money and without price." But the donor purchased it for me at a tremendous sacrifice. I am not holding it for speculation, since the title is not transferable. It is not a vacant lot.

For more than half a century I have been sending materials, out of which the Great Architect and Builder of the Universe has been building a home for me, a home which will never be remodeled nor repaired, because it will suit me perfectly, individually, and will never grow old. Termites can never undermine its foundations, for they rest upon the Rock of Ages. Fire cannot destroy it. Floods cannot wash it away. No locks nor bolts will ever be placed on its doors, for no vicious person can ever enter that Land where my dwelling stands, now almost completed and almost ready for me to enter in and abide in peace eternally, without fear of being ejected.

There is a valley of deep shadows between the place where I live in California and that to which I shall journey in a very short time. I cannot reach my home in that city of gold without passing through this dark valley of shadows; but I am not afraid, because the best Friend I ever had went through the same valley long, long ago and drove away all its gloom. He has stuck by me through thick and thin since we first became acquainted fifty-five years ago, and I hold His promise in printed form that He will never forsake me nor leave me alone. He will be with me as I walk through the valley of shadows, and I shall not lose my way when He is with me.

I hope to hear your sermon on Heaven next Sunday from my home in Los Angeles, but I have no assurance that I shall be able to do so. My ticket to Heaven has no date marked for the journey, no return coupon, and no permit for baggage. Yes, I am all ready to go, and I may not be here while you are talking next Sunday—but I shall meet you Over There some day.

Jesus Christ said: "I go to prepare a place for you. And if I go and prepare a place for you, I will come again, and receive you unto myself; that where I am, there ye may be also. . . . I am the Way, the Truth, and the Life; no man cometh unto the Father, but by me."

On one occasion *Dwight L. Moody*, the great American evangelist, said,

Some day you will read in the papers that D. L. Moody of East Northfield is dead. Don't you believe one word of it! At that moment I shall be more alive than I am now. I shall have gone up higher, that's all—out of this old clay tenement into a house that is immortal; a body that death cannot touch, that sin cannot taint, a body fashioned like His glorious body. I was born of the flesh in 1837. I was born of the Spirit in 1856. That which is born of the flesh may die. That which is born of the Spirit will live for ever.

The death of *John Wesley*, the father of Methodism, occurred in his room on City Road, London. The end was very beautiful. No pain, only a growing sense of weakness, and a tranquil acceptance of the inevitable. He slept much and spoke little, but sometimes the dying flame flickered up, and the inner light that had changed the face of England glowed with its old intensity. One afternoon before he died, he surprised his friends by bursting into song:

I'll praise my Maker while I've breath;
And when my voice is lost in death
Praise shall employ my nobler powers;
My days of praise shall ne'er be past,
While life and thought and being last,
Or immortality endures.

Happy the man whose hopes rely
On Israel's God! He made the sky,
And earth and seas, with all their train;
His truth for ever stands secure;
He saves the oppressed, He feeds the poor,
And none shall find His promise vain.

He sang two verses and then sank back exhausted. Later in the day, when weakness overcame him, by a supreme effort he marshaled his ebbing strength and gave the message that was to become the watchword of Methodism, *"The best of all is, God is with us."*

How beautiful to be with God!
When earth is fading like a dream,

And from this mist-circled shore,
We launch upon the unknown stream.

No doubt, no fear, no anxious care,
But comforted by staff and rod,
In the faith-brightened hour of death,
How beautiful to be with God!

I will not fear to launch my bark
Upon the darkly rolling flood,
'Tis but to pierce the mist—and then
How beautiful to be with God!

Notes

1. *Living Today* Presbyterian Church of Australia, (Melbourne: August, 1991), 16.
2. Robert E. Speer, *Seeking the Mind of Christ* (New York: Revell, 1926), 181.
3. G. P. Tasker, "Immortality," *Evangelical Christian* (Toronto: April 1943), 158.
4. J. I. Packer, *The Apostles' Creed* (Wheaton, Ill.: Tyndale House, 1986), 61.
5. Ibid., 61.
6. Mark Twain, *Letters from the Earth* (New York: Fawcett, 1964), 17.
7. Charles F. Ball, *Heaven* (Wheaton, Ill.: Victor, 1980), 20.
8. David Winter, *Hereafter* (Wheaton, Ill.: Harold Shaw, 1972), 22.
9. J. H. Jowett, *Apostolic Optimism* (New York: Richard R. Smith, n. d.), 171.
10. Alfons Deeken, *Growing Old and How to Cope with It* (New York: Paulist, 1972), 98.
11. W. Graham Scroggie, *What about Heaven?* (Glasgow: Pickering and Inglis, n. d.), 93.
12. John Mac Arthur, Jr., *Heaven* (Chicago: Moody Press, 1988), 19.
13. William Hendriksen, *The Bible on the Life Hereafter*, (Grand Rapids: Baker, 1975), 66.
14. Robert E. Speer, *Jesus and Our Human Problems* (New York: Revell, 1946), 178.
15. Thomas Hewitt, *Epistle to the Hebrews* (London: InterVarsity, 1960), 189.
16. John Gilmore, *Probing Heaven: Key Questions on the Hereafter* (Grand Rapids: Baker, 1989).

17. John Gilmore, *Probing Heaven: Key,* 141.

18. Millard J. Erickson, *Christian Theology* (Grand Rapids: Baker, 1985), 639.

19. Augustus H. Strong, *Systematic Theology* (Philadelphia: Judson Press, 1907), 662.

20. Glen Cupitt, article in *The Reaper* (Auckland, New Zealand, May 1973), 14.

21. Charles F. Ball, *Heaven,* 25.

22. Paige Patterson, *Heaven* (Wheaton, Ill.: Tyndale House, 1991), 124.

23. A. B. Fowler, "Heaven" in *Zondervan Pictorial Bible Dictionary,* 784.

24. Alexander Maclaren, *Gospel of St. John* (New York: George H. Doran, n. d.), 264.

25. F. W. Boreham, *A Casket of Cameos* (London: Epworth, 1924), 277.

26. Rudolf Bultmann, *Kerygma and Myth* (New York: Harper and Row, 1961), 5.

27. Rene Pache, *The Future Life* (Chicago: Moody Press, 1962), 68.

28. W. Graham Scroggie, *What about Heaven?,* 114.

29. Millard J. Erickson, *Christian Theology,* 1233.

30. W. Graham Scroggie, *What about Heaven?,* 112.

31. G. Campbell Morgan, *The Gospel of Luke* (London: Marshall, Morgan, and Scott, n. d.), 197.

32. John Mac Arthur, Jr., *Heaven,* 114–115.

33. Leon Morris, *First Corinthians* (London: InterVarsity, 1958), 28.

34. A. T. Robertson, *Word Pictures of the New Testament* (New York: Harper and Brothers, 1933), 372.

35. Robert H. Mounce, *The Book of Revelation* (Grand Rapids: Eerdmans, 1977), 110.

36. William Hendriksen, *The Bible on the Life Hereafter.*

37. John Mac Arthur, Jr., *Heaven*, 107.

38. Rene Pache, *The Future Life*, 364.

39. Charles F. Ball, *Heaven*, 69.

40. G. H. Lang, *The Revelation of Jesus Christ* (London: Oliphants, 1945), 334.

41. John Gilmore, *Probing Heaven*, 380.

42. Rene Pache, *The Inspiration and Authority of Scripture* (Chicago: Moody Press, 1970), 18.

43. W. Graham Scroggie, *What about Heaven?*, 108.

44. William Hendriksen, *More Than Conquerors* (Grand Rapids: Baker, 1982), 198.

45. Edward M. Bounds, *Glimpses of Heaven* (Pittsburgh: Whittaker, 1985), 31.

46. Wilbur M. Smith, *Wycliffe Bible Commentary* (Chicago: Moody Press, 1962), 1521.

47. G. H. Lang, *The Revelation of Jesus Christ*, 368.

48. William Hendriksen, *More Than Conquerors*, 197.

Note to the Reader

The publisher invites you to share your response to the message of this book by writing Discovery House Publishers, Box 3566, Grand Rapids, MI 49501, USA. For information about other Discovery House books, music, or videos, contact us at the same address or call 1-800-653-8333. Find us on the Internet at http://www.dhp.org/ or send e-mail to books@dhp.org.